Feminism and Gender Research in Japan

There is a large gap between Japan's ranking on indicators of economic development and on indicators of gender equality. This book helps us to understand why.

The chapters in this volume illuminate important dimensions of gender inequality in Japan – in relation to class, and in comparison to other countries. The book considers the relation of gender inequality to neoliberal policies, and the implications of gender inequality for social reproduction. It demonstrates the ways in which leading Japanese scholars are debating and analysing these issues, in dialogue with feminist economists from Mexico and UK.

The chapters in this book were originally published in *The Japanese Political Economy.*

Diane Elson is Emeritus Professor in the Department of Sociology at the University of Essex. She has published widely on gender and development. She was awarded the Leontief Prize for Advancing Frontiers of Economic Thought, 2016, and the International Book Prize, Japan Society of Political Economy, 2018.

Feminism and Gender Research in Japan

Edited by
Diane Elson

Routledge
Taylor & Francis Group
LONDON AND NEW YORK

First published 2023
by Routledge
4 Park Square, Milton Park, Abingdon, Oxon OX14 4RN

and by Routledge
605 Third Avenue, New York, NY 10158

Routledge is an imprint of the Taylor & Francis Group, an informa business

British Library Cataloguing in Publication Data
A catalogue record for this book is available from the British Library

ISBN13: 978-1-032-34499-7 (hbk)
ISBN13: 978-1-032-34500-0 (pbk)
ISBN13: 978-1-003-32244-3 (ebk)

DOI: 10.4324/9781003322443

Typeset in Minion Pro
by Newgen Publishing UK

Publisher's Note
The publisher accepts responsibility for any inconsistencies that may have arisen during the conversion of this book from journal articles to book chapters, namely the inclusion of journal terminology.

Contents

Citation Information

The following chapters were originally published in *The Japanese Political Economy*. When citing this material, please use the original citations and page numbering for each article, as follows:

Chapter 1
Why do Japanese women suffer from the low status?: The impact of neo-liberalist reform on gender
Chizuko Ueno
The Japanese Political Economy, volume 47, issue 1 (2021), pp. 9–26

Chapter 2
Impact of Marxist feminism on Japanese women's movement: Focusing on the domestic labor debates
Kumiko Ida
The Japanese Political Economy, volume 47, issue 1 (2021), pp. 27–43

Chapter 3
Gender equality, paid and unpaid care and domestic work: Disadvantages of state-supported marketization of care and domestic work
Sumika Yamane
The Japanese Political Economy, volume 47, issue 1 (2021), pp. 44–63

Chapter 4
Development, gender, and asymmetries between Mexico and Japan
Alicia Girón
The Japanese Political Economy, volume 47, issue 1 (2021), pp. 64–81

Chapter 5
Intersections of gender and class in the distribution of income
Diane Elson
The Japanese Political Economy, volume 44, issue 1–4 (2018), pp. 7–24

Chapter 6

The reproductive crisis in neoliberal capitalism: Commenting on D. Elson's recent paper
Makoto Itoh
The Japanese Political Economy, volume 47, issue 1 (2021), pp. 82–94

Notes on Contributors

Diane Elson, Department of Sociology, University of Essex, Colchester, UK.

Alicia Girón, UNAM, Coyoacan, Mexico.

Kumiko Ida, Graduate School of Humanities and Sustainable System Sciences, Osaka Prefecture University, Sakai, Japan.

Makoto Itoh, Department of Economics, The University of Tokyo, Tokyo, Japan.

Chizuko Ueno, Graduate School of Humanities and Sociology, The University of Tokyo, Tokyo, Japan.

Sumika Yamane, The Faculty of Humanities and Social Sciences, Jissen Women's University, Hino, Japan.

Introduction: Feminism and Gender Research in Japan

Diane Elson

This book was initiated in an international symposium at Musashi University in 2019 at which I gave a keynote lecture on "Intersections of gender and class in the distribution of income", drawing on my paper first published in *The Japanese Political Economy* Special Issue on 'Is a Feminist Perspective Necessary for Understanding the Economy?', and now included as Chapter 5 in this book. It has been a pleasure to get to know more about the interesting research on gender inequality in Japan and the views of Japanese scholars. The articles in this book illuminate important dimensions of gender inequality in Japan in comparison to other countries; their relation to neoliberal policies; their implications for social reproduction; and the ways in which Japanese scholars are debating and analysing these issues, in dialogue with feminist economists from Mexico and UK.

In Chapter 1 Chizuko Ueno considers the low status of women in Japan in the context of neoliberal reform and argues for social change to create an economy in which care is given a high value. In Chapter 2 Kumiko Ida discusses the domestic labour debate in Japan, showing that it originated before translation of Western debates on this topic, and argues that by displacing the patriarchal concept of labour it empowered women. In Chapter 3 Sumika Yamane critiques policies to reduce the burden of women's unpaid care and domestic work through state-supported marketisation of care and domestic work, comparing Sweden and Japan. In Chapter 4 Alicia Giron compares gender gaps in Japan with those in Mexico, arguing that economic growth does not automatically reduce gender gaps, and that specific policies are required. In Chapter 5 Diane Elson contextualises the position of Japan in the intersections of gender and class inequality in developed economies. In Chapter 6 Makoto Itoh comments on the application of a 'gender lens' to rising economic inequalities under neoliberal capitalism and discusses the crisis of social reproduction in Japan.

Here I take up some of the key issues that they analyse.

1. Gender inequality in Japan

It is startling to learn of the large gap between Japan's ranking on indicators of economic development and on indicators of gender equality. Japan is a high-income country, ranking globally at 19th position in terms of Gross National Income per capita in 2018 (UNDP 2019, 300). However, as Ueno notes, Japan's ranking on the Global Gender Gap Index is low and falling: ranking 101st in

2015 and 121st in 2020. As Giron discusses, while in 2006 Japan was ranked at a similar level to Mexico, a fellow member of OECD and APEC, but with a much lower per capita income, by 2020 Mexico had climbed to 25th place. This was not because the Mexican economy had grown faster than the Japanese economy over this period: in fact, per capita income grew faster in Japan. Giron's comparison shows that achievement of high levels of national income do not necessarily translate into greater gender equality.

One reason why Mexico has done better than Japan in rankings on the Global Gender Gap Index is that, as Giron notes, it has adopted effective policies to equalise the representation of women and men in the political sphere. Japan has not adopted such policies and as Ueno notes, women are only 10.5% members of the Diet. She also raises the question of what equal representation is for – is it a goal in its own right or a tool to achieve social change?

However, lack of women elected representatives is not the only reason for Japan's poor performance. As Ueno demonstrates, Japan has constructed a gendered labour market in which women's position is very inferior to that of men. The gender wage gap in Japan is only higher in two other OECD countries, Estonia and South Korea. There is a higher gender wage gap in Japan than in Mexico: Giron cites OECD data which shows that while the gender wage gap has fallen in both countries, the gap in Japan is double that in Mexico.

Ueno's detailed analysis shows how Japan's labour market has been stratified into regular and irregular workers, with more than half of all female workers irregular but only a fifth of male workers. In 2019, irregular workers got only about two thirds the pay of regular workers, even when they did the same work. Though women's labour force participation in Japan has risen to comparatively high levels, women are structurally disadvantaged in the labour market. Ueno shows how the introduction of the Equal Employment Opportunity Law in 1985 was circumvented by companies by placing most women and men in different job categories, which hindered women from claiming equal treatment, as this was only possible if women were in the same job category of men. This is a clear example of what I had in mind when I claim in Chapter 5 that overt patriarchy has been replaced in developed countries by more subtle, obscured, forms of patriarchy. Ueno also argues that male- dominated labour unions colluded with employers and did not try to organize irregular workers. Ueno's account of the creation of a highly gendered labour market helps us to understand a phenomenon also noted by Itoh: the fall in share of labour in national income in Japan over the same period that female labour force participation rose. As I have argued more generally in Chapter 5, a somewhat similar process was at work in many other high-income economies, driven by structural changes linked to globalisation and technical change. Increased female labour force participation was not in itself responsible for the falling share of labour. It was the creation of highly unequal gendered labour markets that facilitated the fall, with the labour market in Japan particularly biased against women.

Women workers have never been entirely passive in response to the unfavourable conditions of their incorporation in the labour market. In the case of Japan, Ida notes that in the 1990s an independent women's labour movement developed and despite all the obstacles, women were able to successfully win a few wage discrimination cases in the 2000s, using the approach of claiming pay equity based on evaluation of the content of different jobs in the same company. This approach (often known as equal pay for work of equal value) has also proved valuable in other countries, such as the USA and UK. But it depends on being able to compare jobs and pay scales operated by one employer. More challenging is to argue for equal pay across sectors of the economy: women everywhere in the world are segregated into sectors with much lower pay than sectors that employ mainly men.

Yamane notes the low pay of workers in care and domestic work both in Japan, and across the world, and refers to ILO research suggesting that an appropriate yardstick for measuring the degree to which these workers are underpaid is the median earnings of other employees in the rest of the economy. Itoh is concerned that 'the feminist demand for equal wage for equal work may imply approval of meritocracy' and 'import into the female labour market differentiated reward for different kinds of complex labour which has never had much objective foundation'. Indeed, many feminists have long warned that definitions of 'skill' are biased against women and argued against the use of male standards to judge wages and skills (e.g., Phillips and Taylor 1980); and Ueno argues more broadly that what feminists like her want is not a society where winners (women equally with men) are rewarded but one that provides good care and ensures dignity.

A more radical approach to equality in the labour market would be to consider the contribution that different kinds of work make to human well-being and to expand the way in which work is evaluated to take account of this. In the context of Covid 19, in many countries many low-paid workers have been classified as 'essential' and required to continue working through lockdowns, while many high-paid workers in sectors like finance and advertising are not classified as 'essential'. This may open up a space for rethinking what wages ought to be, and even help to challenge the very high salaries paid to CEOs, which Piketty rightly said are not based on objective contributions but on social norms (and social power) (Piketty 2014). We may recall that Marx argued that there is a 'moral and historical element' in the determination of wages (Marx 1887, 1974). In a capitalist economy these elements operate, like so much else, 'behinds the backs' of people. In a democratic egalitarian economy, they would be made visible and subject to participatory debate and agreement. The underpaid care and domestic worker would be paid more than the financial trader and the advertising executive. However, the path towards such an economy is complex, and feminists have to begin the fight from where they stand, supporting legal cases for equal pay for work of equal value, while broadening the concept of what counts as 'equal value', and supporting many other strategies to raise the pay of low-paid women and reduce the pay of highly paid but 'inessential' workers.

2. Unpaid care and domestic work

All the papers make reference to the unequal gender distribution of unpaid care and domestic work as a foundation for other gender inequalities. Ida discusses feminist and Marxist debates in Japan on the role of 'housewives' in the capitalist economic system. These debates originated in the 1960s, and developed further in the 1970s, predating the translation into Japanese of Western writings on these topics in the 1980s.

An interesting early example of Japanese analysis is provided by Tanaka (1971) who suggested that housewives were forced into the position of maids in the household but also played the role of a slave trader 'who refreshes a man who has been worn out … to send him back to the market as a labour power commodity'. I agree with Tanaka that it is important to look at the social relations of production within which housewives work but think the validity of her analogies is limited. There are some similarities but also important differences between housewives and maids. Housewives are not paid wages by their husbands – indeed a key aspect of coercive control that husbands exercise over wives in many contexts is denying their wife access to money. Housewives are legally bound to their husbands and divorce may be very difficult but they also tend to enjoy higher social status and levels of consumption than maids, but the latter may be freer to leave and get another job (depending on their legal status if they are migrants). The analogy with a slave trader is similarly limited: most importantly, the wife does not own the labour power of her husband. It is not she who sells the labour power but he. In capitalism, labour power is not like livestock. It is not produced as a commodity but only becomes a commodity at the point of sale to an employer.

As Ida recounts, the question of whether housework does or does not produce 'value' in the Marxist sense has been subject of intense (and sometimes acrimonious) debate between and among feminists and Marxists in both Japan and the West. In my view, disagreements have often stemmed from not distinguishing between use-value (concrete, specific valuable goods and services) and value (the abstract equivalence of goods and services in the extraction of profit). It is important to recognise that the time spent on unpaid care and domestic labour is not subject to the same competitive processes that shape the use and amount of labour time in capitalist production, reducing it to necessary abstract labour time, in which labourers and labour time are made interchangeable and commensurate in a process that is neither transparent nor democratic (Elson, 1979, 2015). My own conclusion is that quite evidently unpaid care and domestic work is not a purely private matter, and is absolutely necessary for the extraction of profit, but it is not helpful to understand this in terms of production of value, because that hides what is specifically different in the social relations in which this work takes place compared to those of wage work in a capitalist workplace. Just think of the differences between how the length and intensity of the working day is determined in these two sites of production: there are pressures and constraints in both, but they operate in different ways, and the opportunities to challenge them are very different. As Ida notes, Japanese feminists have drawn attention to the role of control over women's sexuality and of domestic violence in the pressures to perform unpaid care and domestic work, something that narrow forms of Marxist economics have ignored.

Recognising the differences between unpaid and paid work does not mean we cannot use a system of social commensuration in which we add together the hours that each person spends per day on unpaid work and paid work to see how long is their total working day. Capitalism does not commensurate labour time in this way, but it has been central to feminist analysis in the last 50 years, looking at labour time from the point of view of the person doing the work, not the person profiting from the work. Under pressure from feminists, many governments have collected time use data, and some have put a shadow wage on time spent on unpaid care and domestic work and compared the resulting aggregate with GDP. As Giron reports, in Japan, the monetary value of unpaid care and domestic work was equivalent to 23.5% of GDP in 2018; and in the case of Japan, 25.7% in 2016. Yamane discusses the pros and cons of different shadow wages, making the point that all the ones that have been used are based on market wages that reflect the low pay of women in unequal labour markets. Thus the results underestimate the importance of the contribution of unpaid care and domestic work to the economy and to society.

A different kind of valuation than the calculus of time and money is valuation in terms of self-worth and social recognition. Ida's analysis suggests that the domestic labour debate in Japan was also important for establishing the conception of women as persons in their own right, making their own contribution to the economy through unpaid work, who should not just be treated as appendages of their husbands, and should enjoy their own social entitlements. She suggests this had an impact when more housewives began to enter the labour market in supporting the development of a women's labour movement that would fight for women's equal rights, as discussed in the preceding section.

The COVID-19 pandemic has intensified demands on women in Japan to provide unpaid care. Ueno refers to new research showing that it is mainly women who take on the extra burden of looking after children when governments require schools to close, and there are similar findings in many countries. The norm persists that it is women who have prime responsibility for unpaid care and domestic work.

3. The crisis of social reproduction

Many high-income economies are experiencing declining birth rates and aging populations, but as Itoh notes, in Japan this process has developed into a slow burning crisis of social reproduction. Japanese women's total fertility rate is now around 1.45, well below the 2.1 required to reproduce the size of the population. Japan's population has already started to decline and is projected to decline by 30% in the 50 years from 2015. As Itoh argues, capital accumulation in Japan is challenged both in terms of the supply of new labour power, and in terms of increased demands on a shrinking population of working age to fund the pensions and health and care services of growing population of retirees.

Ueno notes that there are differences in fertility rates in high-income countries and argues these are linked to the different systems for organising the provision of care. She analyses this in terms of three types: Type A double earner households with care provision by the public sector, as in Scandinavia; Type B double earner households with commodification of care in the market, as in Singapore and USA; Type C male breadwinner households with unpaid care provided by women at home, as in Japan and southern European countries. Fertility rates are highest in Type A countries, followed by Type B countries; and lowest in Type C countries. She looks at fertility as an indicator of the vision of the future held by women and men of reproductive age and concludes: 'we can say that the male breadwinner model gives them the least hope for future society'. She calls for a society where care is highly valued and equally shared.

Both Giron and Yamane refer to recent efforts by the Japanese government to develop publicly financed care services. Giron notes a rapid growth in day care facilities, though there is still considerable unmet need. Yamane provides an analysis of Long Term Care Insurance, showing how though the system is largely funded from taxation, it outsources the provision of care services for the elderly to the private sector. This state-supported marketisation has driven down the already low pay of care workers, and driven down the quality of care, for instance by reducing the time allowed for a home care visit. As Yamane notes, there is a similar system in the UK, which also prioritises 'cost-effectiveness' over quality of conditions and pay for workers and quality of care for users of the service.

Yamane also discusses state-supported marketisation of domestic work in Sweden through introduction of tax allowances for the expense of hiring a paid domestic worker to provide cleaning and care services to the household. She argues for systems of paid care provision that are based on equality between the workers and users in terms of dignity and rights to replace a consumerist model of marketized services. Among the strategies to achieve this, she suggests the governments must ensure that workers enjoy improved pay by directly setting wages; and that efforts to improve quality of services should not rest on competition between different providers, but on better training, and public inspections of companies that provide care and domestic services . There should also be support for the development of trade unions and cooperatives of care and domestic workers. Itoh calls for similar strategies, emphasizing the need for a 'really democratic socialization of the reproduction of labour-power from the grassroots in ways that go beyond the limitations of 20th century statist nationalistic models'.

A civil society Commission on a Gender Equal Economy that I chaired in the UK in 2020 discussed many similar issues and concluded that the whole basis of the economy needs to be changed away from pursuit of short-term financial gain and economic growth to focus on achievement of equality, human well-being and environmental sustainability and creation of a Caring Economy (Commission on a Gender Equal Economy 2020). This means changes not only to the reproduction of labour power but also to the labour process throughout the economy, including breaking down the division between long working hours for men, and part-time working hours for women, so that there is a 'normal working week' of around 30 hours for both. This would allow men to participate much more in unpaid care and domestic work, as a younger generation of men is beginning to do. To achieve gender equality men's lives need to change as well as women's, and care not capital needs to shape the economy.

References

Commission on a Gender Equal Economy. 2020. *Creating a Caring Economy: A Call to Action.* London: Women's Budget Group. https://wbg.org.uk/wp-content/uploads/2020/10/WBG-Report-v10.pdf

Elson, Diane. Ed. 1979. *Value. The Representation of Labour in Capitalism.* London: CSE Books. Reissued 2015. London: Verso.

Marx, Karl. 1887. English translation 1974. *Capital* Volume 1. London: Lawrence and Wishart.

Piketty, Thomas. 2014. *Capital in the Twenty First Century.* Cambridge, MA: Harvard University Press.

Phillips, Anne and Taylor, Barbara. 1980. "Sex and Skill: Notes Towards a Feminist Economics". *Feminist Review* 6:79–88.

Tanaka, Mitsui. 1971. "Chiisana Hibana mo Kouya wo Yakitsukusu" [Even Small Sparks Burn the Wilderness]. *Kouzou* 101:8297. Tokyo: Keizaikozo-sha.

UNDP. 2019. *Human Development Report 2019.* New York: UNDP.

Why do Japanese women suffer from the low status?: The impact of neo-liberalist reform on gender

Chizuko Ueno

ABSTRACT
The global ranking of Japan's Gender Gap Index is 121st among 153 countries in 2020, disproportionally low compared with Japan's GDP ranked at the third. This paper explores the structural background and the historical path-dependency why Japanese women are confined at the low status. The so-called Japanese style management, once considered as a success model, is responsible for this gender inequality, which strongly sticks to the male breadwinner model. The paper also explains who pays the cost of gender discrimination, and its historical outcome in the international community in the comparative context. With the lack of outsourcing alternatives of women's care burden, namely, neither socialization of care service in the public sector at the cost of high tax burden, nor commodification of care service in the market at the cost of cheap migrant labor, gender serves as a functional equivalent with class and race in other societies, which accordingly keep Japanese women at the bottom of labor market. In addition, the paper proves the negative impact of the COVID-19 pandemic on women, particularly on single mothers, where the existing gap is widened and accelerated at the time of crisis.

Introduction

The global ranking of Japan's Gender Gap Index (GGI) is going lower and lower year by year. It is 101st in 2015, 114th in 2016, 118th in 2017, 110th in 2018, 114th in 2019 and then 121st among 153 countries in the recent year, 2020 (World Economic Forum). Compared with Japan's GDP, which is ranked the third next to the USA and China, Japan's ranking of GGI is disproportionally low.

This paper explores the structural background and the historical path-dependency why Japanese women are confined at the low status and who is responsible for this gender inequality. The paper also explains who pays the cost of gender discrimination, and its historical outcome in the international community in the comparative context.

The low global ranking of Japan's GGI

The GGI consists of four indices such as health, education, politics and economy. In the 2020 ranking While Japanese women's situation in health and education is not so bad (40th in health, and 65th in education), the latter two are surprisingly low.

The women's representation in the Diet is 10.5% at the latest national election in 2017, ranked 144th, lower than the total global ranking, and the economic status is ranked 115th, also lower than the total ranking. Compared with the global ranking of Japan's GDP, which is third next to the USA and China, Japan's GGI is disproportionally poor.

This does not necessarily mean the Japanese women's situation is getting worse. It means Japan is very slow to change in the gender aspect, while other countries have made a progress. Japanese government received severe recommendations several times from the UN Committee on Elimination of all Forms of Discrimination against Women (CEDAW) which urged Japan to make more efforts, as if it had neglected the UN Treaty against gender discrimination[1]. Japan is left far behind in the global trend and then, why?

Wage gap by gender

The Low economic status mainly comes from the wage gap by gender. Though it is getting better to reach the level as much as 75.5% of the male wage in 2019, which is the second worst from the bottom next to Korea among OECD countries. When the UN decade for women started in 1975, the wage gap was 63:100 as women to men, it has reached up to 75:100 in nearly half a century since then, but it is still the lowest among G7 countries. Though it was indeed improved, the change is very slight.

The major reason for Japanese women's low economic status comes from irregular employment. Though wage gap by gender among the same category of workers is becoming smaller, wage gap between regular workers and irregular workers is fixed at the high level. It is so wide as to reach the level not to be justified in the economic reasons.

Irregular employment is highly gendered. As seen in Figure 1, there is an increasing number of irregular workers among women. By the year 2014, irregular workers have consisted of 37.4% of all workers, with 21.8% among male workers, and 56.7% among female workers. Among all the irregular workers, nearly 70% are women.

The problem with irregular works is first the lack of job security and secondly the disproportionally low wage with no rational reasons. A gender specialist, Osawa (1993), calls it "status discrimination." Irregular workers are paid about a half or two-third of regular workers on an hourly basis

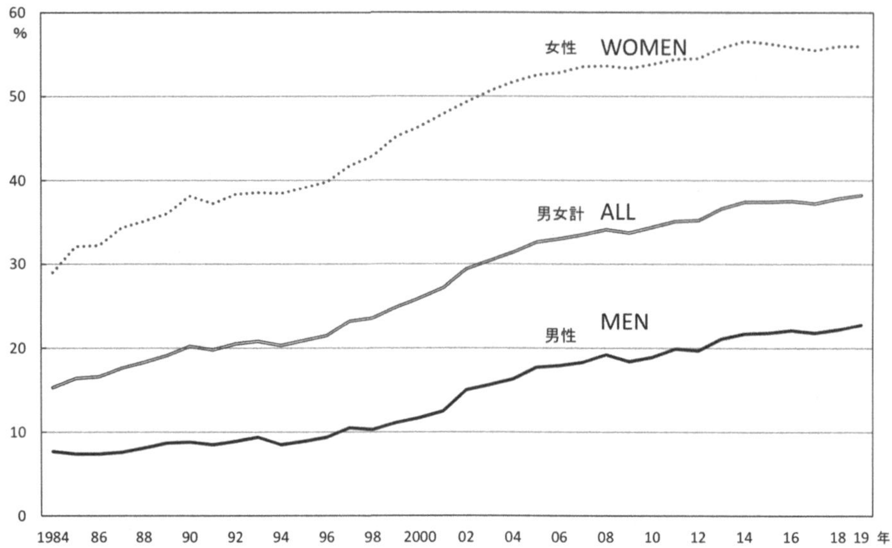

Figure 1. Irregular employment rate 1984–2019 (Source: The Japan Institute of Labor Policy and Training).

though they do the similar jobs, and earn barely less than the survival level even when they work full time[2].

This low wage has been excused by employers as the supplementary income for the household economy by married women. The jobs for pin money such as parttime jobs, were made to fit married women, so as to exploit them.

Until the early 1990s, it was likely the case that most part-time workers were married and middle-aged who returned to the labor market in the post-nurturing stage, but from that time on, many single women, both unmarried women and divorced single mothers, joined the irregular labor market to support their life as household heads. Later men and foreigners also joined this irregular labor market, which resulted in the widening class gap.

Back in the 1970s Japan was relatively the equal society with the income gap between the top and the bottom at the second lowest next to Sweden among OECD countries. It was called "the Middle-Class Society" where more than 80% of the nations answered yes to the question whether they belonged to the middle class. In 50 years, this is no longer the case: today income gap in Japan is ranked the second biggest next to the USA among all OECD countries. The relative poverty rate reached 15.6% next to the worst 16.8% of the USA among OECD countries (2015), so that some sociologists call the Japanese society, "a new class society" (Hashimoto 2018; Yoshikawa 2018; Amemiya 2018). The Marxian term, "class" came back to the sociological analysis in the 2000s. Poverty is becoming more visible among irregular workers especially at the crisis of COVID-19 pandemic, because they lose their jobs.

Historical background

Tracing back the history, the neo-liberalist reform in Japan started in the 1980s. It has introduced a wide range of irregular workers in the process of deregulation of existing labor regulations one after another so as to cut down the wage. Throughout the same period, labor share of national income has also decreased.

In the year 1985, when the Equal Employment Opportunity Law (EEOL) was made, the first Labor Dispatch Law was also made. Up until then, dispatch business[3] had been long considered against public interest, and banned for profit-making. Accordingly, the Public Employment Security Office helped businesses that had vacancies to find workers, and helped people who were looking for employment to find a job, known as Hello Work. In this year, labor dispatch was made possible for profit making, which invited private corporations to join this business. In the beginning, while starting in the midst of boosted Bubble Economy in the mid-eighties, dispatch workers were limited to highly specialized jobs, and relatively better paid. Later on, the process of deregulation took place year by year, and today dispatch works become available for almost all kinds of jobs even on the day's work.

Dispatch workers are registered workers to the dispatch business with zero hours contract. There is no guarantee for them to get another job when their contract is terminated. The law requires employers to provide them with fulltime permanent employment after a certain period of time (three years by the reformed Labor Dispatch Law in 2018), as it is considered as a regular post. Though the reformed law aims at securing jobs for irregular workers in theory, in practice it gives employers to replace them every three years. This three years' rule destroys not only job security but also accumulation of job training as well as career plan for irregular workers, mostly women. Such a negative impact was predicted by gender studies scholars, who claimed that this disadvantage was a part of planned policy impact. Though it is a loss for employers to replace experienced workers with new ones, they choose to save wages by so doing.

Among irregular workers, in addition to dispatch workers, there are other categories of employment such as part-time, temporary, and contract workers who are directly employed by corporations. They are all low-paid work with no job security, namely disposable labor force made to fit women and foreign residents[4]. Japanese corporations were squeezed at the corner as to cut down the labor cost in the more competitive global market, but they tried to secure male breadwinners' employment at the price of women's low wage.

The problem with irregular employment is first the low wage, and secondly the lack of job security. Though the minimum wage is applied to them, the wage gap between regular employment and irregular one is about two thirds in 2019[5], even when they do the same work. Employers take advantage of difference in job categories for cutting down the labor cost.

Service economy also helped women to participate in the irregular labor market. Irregular workers consist of nearly 50% of retail industry and restaurants, and 35% of inter-personal service industries such as care businesses (2019). In the same period of time, irregular workers have also increased in the public sector so as to reach almost 25% of public servants, known as "working poors" made by the public sector. It is a real irony that career consultants working at Hello Work, or the public employment security office, have no job security, because they are themselves irregular workers.

This series of deregulation was called "Big Ban of Employment" in Japanese English, or namely disintegration of employment, which has in fact destroyed job security for many workers. This particular year, 1985, was retrospectively called the year of inauguration of widening class gap, or eventually, women's poverty (Ueno 2013).

The deceptive trade

The EEOL did not serve to help women. Right after the implementation of the law, women's employment was seemingly increased. But later it turned out to be simply an effect of boosted economy in the late 1980s. After the Bubble Economy was collapsed in 1991, women's employment went worse. Despite the law, the gender gap in employment became widened. The law did not help to protect women's employment in the recession, which was predicted by most gender specialists and activists, who stood against the making of the law, because the law did not promise effective gender equality.

At the time of law making, I myself called EEOL "a deceptive trade between protection and equality." Up until then, the Labor Standard Act allowed women to have paid menstrual leave, and protections from long working hours, midnight shift and dangerous, harmful jobs in the name of protection of motherhood. At the time of making the law, the employers' associations proposed forcible alternatives "either equality or protection." Instead of losing existing protections of motherhood guaranteed by the Labor Standard Act, what women workers gained was a nominal equality in recruitment and promotion with no penalty clauses.

Major corporations tried to undermine the law by introducing the double track system between career track and non-career track, assigning all men and a few women on the former and the rest of majority of women on the latter. By so doing they successfully replaced the gender-based placement with the one based on the job category. Thus, employers survived the EEOL without changing themselves. Theoretically the EEOL is the law which makes possible for women to claim equal treatment as far as she belongs to the same job category as men. Once she is employed in the different job category, she loses the right to claim discrimination against gender, which many women workers had fought for until then. Though EEOL created a handful of women on the career track, Osawa described the law as tailor-made, which meant that only women dressed in tailored men's suits could survive in the workplace.

The real irony lies in the fact the law had nothing to do with the increasing number of irregular workers, because it is not applicable to them. Thirty years after implementation of the EEOL, women members in the Science Council of Japan, including myself, organized a symposium open to public, with the title, "Has the EEOL turned out to be a swan?" Thirty years are long enough to evaluate its policy impact on gender. This strange title suggested that the law, once born as an ugly duckling, had eventually turned to be a beautiful swan, that is to say, effective to help women. I was one of the keynote speakers at the symposium, and my answer was simply No, saying it turned out to be a decoy of neo-liberalism.

Villains and accomplices

Then who is responsible for this deregulation, which accompanied the destruction of employment? There are villains and accomplices.

In 1995, in the midst of the depression called "the ice age" for job hunters, the Japanese Business Federation (Japan's biggest and most influential organization of corporate managers) published a report, "The Japanese Style Management in the New Era," (1995) in which they proposed new style of employments in the following three categories: first one is that on the career track, conventional as before, as to be slimmed down; second is the highly specialized professionals, as to be outsourced: the third is the flexible labor such as part-time, dispatch, temporary and contract workers, namely the reserve army of the labor force, disposable on business cycle. Women and youth, or those latecomers to the labor market, were thrown into this irregular labor market from the beginning. Though women's labor force participation has increased throughout the period, it took place mainly in the irregular labor market.

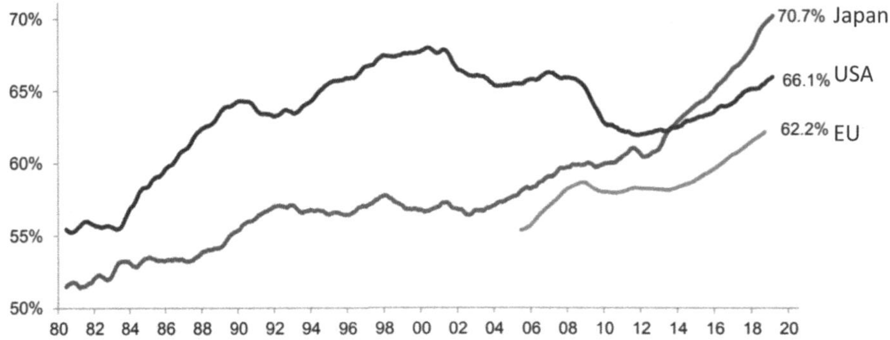

Figure 2. Japanese Women's Labor Force Participation (Source: OECD).

The employer's association worked together with conservative politicians and bureaucrats to promote the deregulation process of employment. There is another accomplice of this disintegration of employment, that is to say, male labor unionists. They were only concerned with their own job security. As far as their status-quo was secured, they did not mind the disadvantage of latecomers, mainly women and youth, who are thrown into the irregular labor market. Major labor unions did not try to organize irregular workers, while their number was increasing.

During the same decades, women's labor force participation has increased. Under the long-lasting recession, double income has become imperative for maintaining the household finance. Now 70% of Japanese women in the productive age join the labor market, which exceeds that of he USA and the EU in number, but nearly six out of ten women workers work at the low wage on the irregular conditions (Figures 2 and 3).

Unfavorable tax system for women

The Japanese tax system strongly supports the male breadwinner model, which allows employers to exploit women. Household heads, mostly male, can receive tax exemption for dependents, as far as their spouses' income is lower than some 10,000 euros. Among married irregular workers, 26% of women (2018) control their working hours to keep their income not to exceed this limit, as they do not want to lose the legal status as dependents.

This tax system is mistakenly called "favorable for married women" but in fact they are their husbands and their employers who benefit from it: first because their husbands do not have to pay the social security cost for their wives as they are covered by their insurance as dependents in the same households: secondly because their employers neither have to cover the social security cost for those irregular workers who remain as dependents. Therefore, this system gives employers a good excuse to keep their wages low.

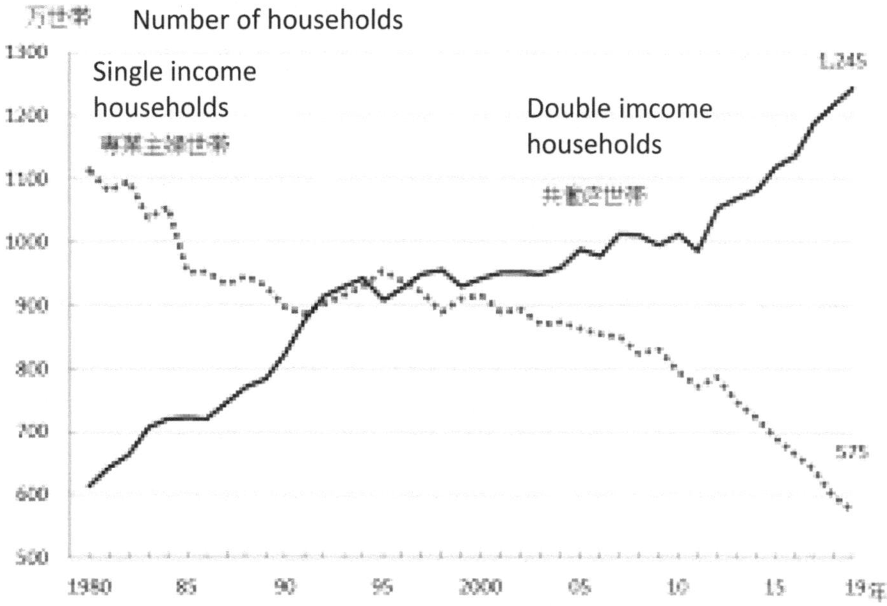

Figure 3. Increase of Double Income Households 1980–2019. Source: The Japan Institute for Labor Policy and Training. https://www.jil.go.jp/kokunai/statistics/timeseries/html/g0212.html.

This tax system strongly discourages married women to work longer hours, and thus, keep them dependent on husbands. As their income is too low to support even a single household, this system acts as a disincentive to divorce, as they would lose all the security as dependents. As far as their husbands' employments are secured, their status as dependents is also secured, which has been called "corporate welfare." This system worked favorable for husband to guarantee to receive care till the end of their life, because the social security and pension system is advantageous for widows, who complete their marriage. Generally speaking, the Japanese tax and social security system is favorable for male household heads, which encourages women to stay in marriage[6].

Never-the-less, this did not help to stop increasing number of divorce among youth, as they become less tolerant of their mistreatment by their husbands. Today one out of three marriages ends up with divorce, which means that young women dare to make an unfavorable decision, even though they are aware of the anticipated poverty of single mother households. In addition to the poor job opportunities for women with children, they have little support from their ex-husbands. Though single parents can receive public child rearing allowance[7] when their annual income is lower than 1.6 million yen, the average income with public allowance is only 2.43 million yen (about 19000 euros) and their poverty rate reaches as much as 51.4% (2018)[8].

Unexpected results

The neoliberalist reform, starting in the 1980s, has brought unexpected results in the following two ways.

First, more men and single women, including single mothers, have entered to the irregular labor market. Male irregular workers were mainly allocated in the manufacturing industry, such as car industry. Female irregular workers mainly join the service industry and clerical jobs. The share of irregular workers is highest in the service industry, nearly at 50% such as restaurants and retail business, and then next highest among service workers such as care workers, not to be replaced with on-line jobs. These irregular workers work for household support but not for supplementary income. Back behind this trend, there is a demographic change, such as late marriage and increasing divorce rate. More women tend to stay out of marriage for longer period of life.

Secondly, those who once entered irregular labor market, were fixed as they were, because the Japanese style management prevents them from changing their job category from irregular to regular. As their parents become old, their children who remained as private dependents in the same household, called a "parasite," also turned middle-aged, and then the former will no longer afford to feed the latter on their small pensions. This is called "8050" problems, meaning parents in the eighties feeding children in the fifties will become in need of care. This demographic outcome was predicted and warned by specialists a long time ago.

The neoliberalist reform resulted in the widening class gap among women between elite women workers and mass of non-elite women workers. In addition to the existing gender gap, the gap among women was also widened, which made women's solidarity more difficult.

Causes and solutions

The neo-liberalist reform was conducted by the consensus of male alliance of politicians, bureaucrats, and employers, and one more additional actor and accomplice, that is to say, male labor unionists. They have stuck to the so-called Japanese style management, which keeps strong breadwinner model.

The Japanese style management is comprised of the following three factors: life-time employment, seniority-based payment and promotion, and in-company unions. This system functioned well at the time of economic growth when full employment was almost achieved. However, it makes it very difficult for dropouts to recover the fulltime employment, once they lose it. Even at the time of economic recovery, it only affects fresh comers in the labor market.

Though these rules refer nothing to gender, it functions systematically and structurally to exclude women from workplaces. We define gender discrimination as follows; when a certain system or a set of rules works disproportionally advantageous or disadvantageous either for a group of men or that of women, it is called gender discriminating. Judging from this definition, the Japanese style management is no doubt gender discriminating.

There is a consensus among sociologists and economists that the Japanese style management is the source of all the evil for gender discrimination (Kawaguchi 2008; Hamaguchi 2015; Ebihara 2012; Nakano 2014; Ueno 2013). The alternative proposal was already made with the following three conditions: first, restriction of long working hours, second, abolishment of seniority system and third, establishment of equal pay for equal work. Never-the-less many economists predict that it is extremely difficult for Japanese corporations to change, as they keep their system in equilibrium with existing rules. A sociologist, Yamaguchi (2017), calls this equilibrium "an inferior equilibrium," but it is hard to change even at a part, because an equilibrium is an equilibrium, no matter how dysfunctional it works. Yamaguchi also points out that the long working hours of management posts functions as the major obstacle against the promotion of women. The result is the vast amount of external diseconomy, in other words, the waste of women's labor power.

Comparative studies

Comparative studies can tell us why Japanese women have to suffer from incomparable difficulties different from those in other societies.

Neo-liberalist reform was a common response to globalization in most industrialized countries. In this process, mobilization of women to the labor market is imperative for neoliberalist reform, due to the decrease of labor force with the low fertility. The main difference between conservative politicians and neoliberalist ones is that the latter would never say women should go back home, because they want women to work as well as to give birth. They are aware that women are the last resource of Japan, which they cannot afford to waste.

In order to mobilize women to the workforce, family responsibility or care burden, which keeps women at home, has to be transferred from women's shoulders to somewhere else.

Reproductive labor, or care work, known as unpaid work, has become visible in the process of gender reconfiguration. Every society has to reproduce itself for sustainability, so that distribution of reproductive cost has become a big question to solve.

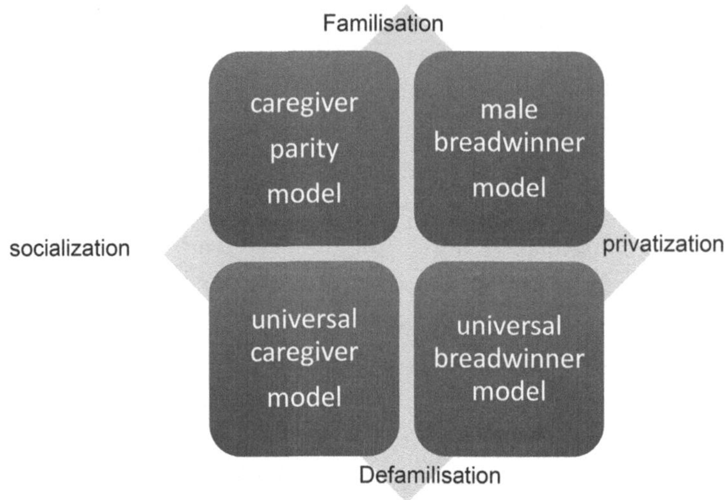

Figure 4. Distribution of care.

The distribution of reproductive labor or care work can take the following two forms; socialization and privatization. The other dimension can also take the following two forms; defamilisation and familisation after Esping-Andersen (1990)[9]. In combination, theoretically there are four types of distribution of care work; first one is the privatized family care, a conventional type; the second one is the family care subsidized by the state with family allowance and tax exemptions; the third one is outsourcing of family care by purchasing the commodified care service in the market; the fourth is outsourcing of care in the public sector by providing public care service. The former two types have been proven gender discriminating, as it tends to fix gender role assignment. It keeps a conventional, conservative patriarchal family.

Frazer (1993) proposed the following four models based on the gender role and welfare system; male breadwinner model, caregiver parity model, universal caregiver model and universal breadwinner model. Her models can be categorized as such seen in the diagram in Figure 4. Familisation of care may work gender indifferently in theory, because it can take a form of egalitarian family, which is least likely the case as far as the wage gap by gender continues. Then caregiver parity model tends to fix women's role as care givers like the breadwinner model. In many countries, male breadwinners receive tax subsidies and other benefits to keep their wives as dependents, so that we can integrate the first two models into one as a male breadwinner model in practice.

After Frazer's model, I make a revised model based on the type of outsourcing of care work. Type A is double earner model with socialization of care in the public sector, applied by Scandinavian countries, such as Sweden,

Norway and Denmark, at the cost of high tax burdens. Though tax payers agree to pay a price for public service, care workers in the public sector are relatively low paid, some of whom are migrant workers. Type B is double earners model with commodification of care in the market. This is the privatized solution, as far as they can afford to purchase domestic service as commodity, when their opportunity cost is higher than the domestic workers. Anglo-Saxon countries as well as several Asian countries such as Singapore and Hong Kong can apply this type with huge class gap in terms of race and class, where cheap migrant labor is available. In these Asian countries, the work-life balance of women is no longer the problem, as they have nannies and maid servants at home from neighboring countries such as the Philippines and Indonesia. Type C is a conventional breadwinner model with privatized care at home at the price of women, applied not only in Japan but also in southern European countries such as Spain, Italy and Greece. In Asia, there is another type of possible solution to be called "Asian type," namely, help by grandparents. This is less likely to be available, as late marriage and late birth have made grandparents older.

Since Japan lacks the first two solutions, neither socialization nor commodification of care, in other words, substantial amount of public care service nor commodified care service by cheap labor in the market, it is women who pay the reproductive cost. In this sense, gender serves as a functional equivalent in Japan, comparable with race and class in other countries, which keeps Japanese women at the bottom in the labor market. This explains why Japanese women suffer from the particular difficulties than women in other countries.

Interestingly enough, these types, A, B, and C end up with difference in fertility. The type A comes at the top, and the type B comes next, and the type C comes at the last with the lowest fertility rate (Figures 5 and 6). If fertility may serve as an index of the vision for the future by individual men and women of the reproductive age, we can say that the male breadwinner model gives them least hope for the future society.

In my book, "Patriarchy and Capitalism" (Ueno 1990, 2008) I named this problem as a question of redistribution of reproductive cost. Even when the unpaid work, once conducted by women at home, is outsourced, either socialized or commodified, care work is still low paid.

Back behind the issue, the last question remains unsolved: at the very end of my book, I wrote as follows: "Why the reproductive labor, such as giving birth, nurturing, caring and tending human being from the beginning to the end of life, remains unvalued? Until this question is solved, women's problems will last forever." (Ueno 1990, 308–309).

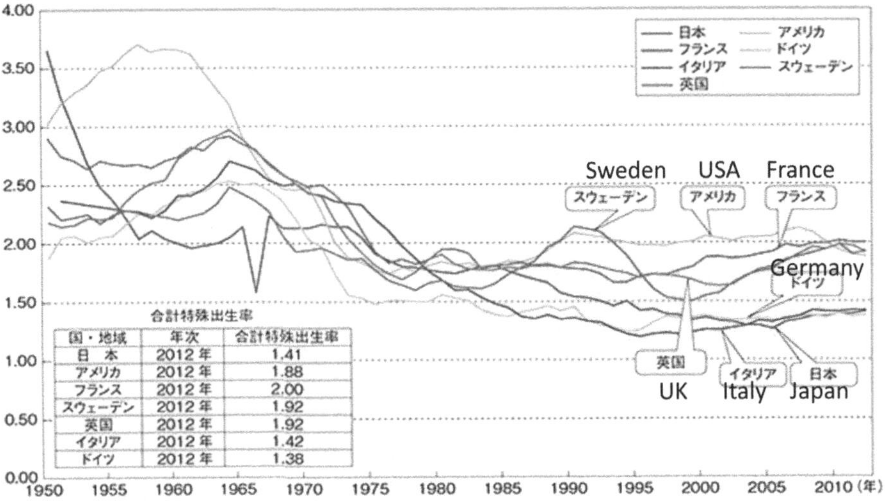

Figure 5. Fertility Rate in Europe (Source: Cabinet Office, 2017).

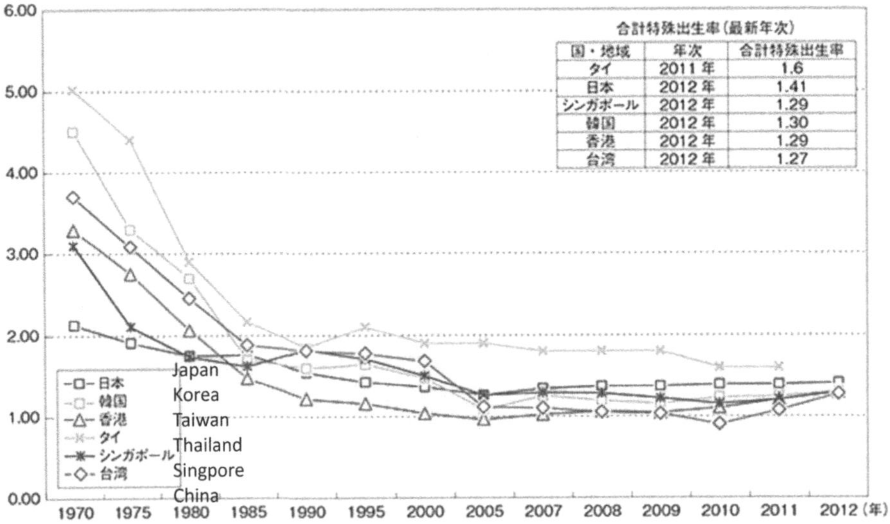

Figure 6. Fertility Rate in Asia (Source: Cabinet Office, 2017).

COVID-19 and its impact on gender

On top of the existing gender gap, the cricis by Covid-19 pandemic has enforced and accelerated the disadvantage to those who were already vulnerable.

The pandemic has brought a serious impact on women workers, who are care givers at home for children and the elderly. The government requirement for closing schools at the nation-wide level has made invisible care work visible. Who cares young children who have no place to go than staying at home? It was always women who sacrifice their work. Ochiai Emiko, a feminist sociologist, quickly conducted on-line research for women with children and found their family burden has been added[10].

The pandemic gave a damage particularly to irregular workers. Due to the continuous legal reform which has made working conditions of irregular workers worse to shorten the period of contact up to one year, half a year and even to the three months, employers can easily terminate their contract every three months without any penalties. They have already experienced June crisis, September crisis, and then anticipate December crisis, because the end of contract comes every three months.

The Japanese government organized research committee on the impact and tasks for women with COVID-19 in September, led by a feminist sociologist, Shirahase Sawako. The committee quickly issued the Urgent Proposals in two months, in which they named current situation, "the Gendered Depression," because women's impact was more serious. According to their report, women's employment suddenly decreased 740,000 from March to April, when the government required school closure at the nationwide level. Compared with decrease of men's employment up to 32,000, the number of women who lost jobs is more than doubled. The major reason is that women's employment is concentrated in the irregular labor market, particularly in the service industry, retail business and restaurants which are the most seriously damaged sectors of industries by the pandemic.

In return to the requirement of school closure, the government offered furlough scheme to cover lost wages to a certain extent, as they can no longer assume that women are jobless. Now more than 60% of the entire households are double income families, where both husband and wives are working. At the beginning, this scheme did not cover self-employed workers. In response to the criticism, the government decided to pay the half of the cost of fulltime employees to freelance and self-employed workers. It did not cover workers in the sexually entertaining businesses neither, but the government changed their policy to include them in response to the public protest. Tough sex work is illegalized in Japan, sex-related business is easy to access by single mothers, known as the last social security.

However, furlough money hardly reached irregular workers, as their employers simply terminated the contracts. Even in the case of regular employment, it is employers who subscribe this scheme, and then there is no guarantee that the money should go to the employees.

The school closure particularly gave a serious impact on single mother family, because they were only one breadwinner and carer in the household. Non Profit Organization, Single Mother's Forum, conducted an intensive survey for its members and published the research report in August[11]. Among their questionnaires, 70% of single mothers answered yes to the question whether the pandemic affected their jobs and income. While 4.5% of fulltime workers lost jobs, 16.1% of irregular workers lost jobs, and then their income by work. Though they receive single mother's allowance from the government, it is not enough to support their household. Even before the pandemic, the annual income of single household is 200 million yen (about 16,000 euros) on the average, lower than the survival level, and the 52% of single mothers live below the poverty line. Only one third of their ex-husband continue to pay child support, since the Japanese civil code does not have a compulsive rule to have them pay. The pandemic have made their life much more difficult. It is important to record and report the reality, what the crisis has brought to people, especially to those vulnerable groups of the society.

The impact of the COVID-19 pandemic is highly gendered. It gives us a depressive prediction that it will widen the class gap as well as the gender gap, and eventually make the Japan's global ranking of GGI lower next year.

Equal representation for what? A goal or a tool?

Women's under-representation has been problematized, and today there is no objection against women's equal participation in all fields of society. Even conservative politicians would give an approval to this policy.

The government set up the goal in figures as "202030," meaning to increase women leaders up to 30% in all the fields by the year 2020. My first response to this action plan was "why not 202050?" However, 30% is still a meaningful figure called "critical mass" which would change the organization culture with the presence of a minority group. In reality the current situation about women leaders in various fields is too poor to reach the goal, so that the government postponed the goal year to ten years ahead by 2030.

Women's under-representation is considered as injustice, so that equal representation itself is considered as social justice. Never-the-less, what can we expect when equal representation is achieved? Is it a goal or a tool? Is women's equal representation a goal for its own sake? Or if it is a tool, a tool for what?

The discourses which justify gender equality are given as the following three answers: first for fairness, second for efficiency, and the last for the social change toward a feminist goal.

First, fairness should be gender indifferent. Equal opportunity and fair competition are the keywords for this. If a woman is given a talent or competence, she should be given a chance equal to men. Liberal feminism supports this fairness. Equal opportunity in fair competition will end up with creating winners and losers, where winners should be rewarded according to his or her achievements, with losers left behind. Fairness in opportunities does not necessarily guarantee the distribution justice in the outcome, where social security for minority people works only as supplementary to the market principle. This discourse nicely fit in professionalism.

The second goal is efficiency of the society (Esping-Andersen 2009). If women's labor power is not utilized by the society, it is called "external waste." This discourse is now mobilized to persuade managers and employers to promote gender equality. Economists are enthusiastic to prove the better performance of the gender equal corporations compared with gender discriminating ones; thus, the former is more efficient than the latter in profit making. Therefore, gender equality is beneficial for employers and then, economically rational in the market. This discourse nicely fits in neoliberalism, which will throw women into more severe competition.

The third and the last discourse is the social change for a feminist goal, which is equal to answer the question what society we feminists want?

Women are still characterized as care givers. If social justice matters, feminism has struggled to seek for the distribution justice of care by gender. Care is a human activity to give birth, nurture, nurse, and tend at the time of death, concerning about the beginning and the end of the life, namely, human reproduction. People in need of care are fallen into dependency. Though women are not dependent by nature, they become dependent when they take a role of carers. Fineman (1995, 2004), a feminist legal theorist, calls it as "secondary dependency" derived from the first dependency. The first dependency originates from people in need, such as children, aged and disabled, but the secondary dependency is derived from the first one for those who care them. Gender role assignment, with women as carer, keeps them from the labor market and make them economically dependent on male breadwinners.

Then is it really a goal for women to get rid of this dependency to be independent equal to men? Many feminist thinkers on care point out the liberalist myth of independent individuals modeled on the healthy adult males, and rather argue that this myth is constructed by forgetting their own dependency. A Japanese feminist political scientist, Okano (2012), defines the modern liberalism as Politics of Oblivion. Human beings are determined to be dependent at the beginning as well as at the end of the life. If women's mobilization to paid labor has made care issues visible, the feminist concern must problematize how our society deals with care. To answer the feminist question is to solve the question of gender distribution justice of care burden. It may not be appropriate to call it simply as a burden, because care can be also a meaningful human activity.

Answering the question what society we want, it is not a society where winners should be rewarded, but one where the dependent and frail will be given good care. I myself define feminism as a thought and practice which aims at the society where the social minorities are treated with dignity as they are.

In this sense, I would argue that feminists have never wished to be male clones so as to join the power game as winners. Ruddick (1989), a feminist philosopher, says that caring experience would serve to learn nonviolence, since caring is a continuous process to refrain oneself from exercising the abuse of power. It is an experience to resist the seduction of power for a long period of time, because care relations are definitely asymmetrical power relations, where players are not interchangeable.

If violence is something to be learned, nonviolence can also be learned. Since the base of security is nonviolence, we should involve men in caring. Men are not naturally violent: they are socialized to be violent, just like women are socialized to be nonviolent, because women are not naturally peace lovers.

Again, back to the first question: equal representation is not a goal for its own sake. Without thinking what society we want through women's equal representation, and what goal we feminists aim at, equal representation will be in vain. Nonviolence is the necessary condition for human security, which should be given priority to the state security. If our goal is a secured society, gender matters greatly.

Notes

1. CEDAW gives recommendations once 3 years to all countries that ratified the Convention on the Elimination of all the forms of Discrimination against Women. Since 2003 Japanese government continuously received almost same contents of recommendations which means that Japan did not change. Among them CEDAW recommended a right for married couple to use separate surnames. This right has not been established until now, and in 2015 the supreme court judged the current civic law as constitutional, which imposed the same surname to a couple.
2. This is the major difference between Japanese irregular workers and European ones, whose income gap is relatively small compared with regular workers.
3. Dispatch business is a business that operates as a labour supply agency, dispatching workers that are registered with it to businesses that have vacancies.
4. The Japanese government has never used the administrative term, "immigrant" in the foreign policy, because they tries to prevent foreign workers from settling down to form a family.
5. The basic survey of wage structure, Ministy of Labor and Welfarer, 2020.
6. Adult children are not eligible for dependents, unless they have special reasons for being unable to work, due to disability, disease, or schooling.

7. The child-rearing allowance stays at relatively low level compared with European countries; 42,000 yen for the first child, 10,000 for the second one and 6000 for the third and so on.
8. The 5th national survey of households with children. The Research Institute of Labor Policy.
9. Esping-Andersen originally uses the terms, familialization and defamilialization, but later a set of terms, familisation and defailisation, has become more common among welfare theorists, so that I follow this terminology, owing to the editors.
10. https://wan.or.jp/article/show/8880
11. "A quick report on the serious impact on single mothers by COVID-19 : A survey of 1800 single mothers' lives" https://note.com/single_mama_pj/n/n83bb1e08b706?fbclid=IwAR0TLltGjx_XQBDr8s9m2sE8wc3ODa8QauXk60SYtAJMq_xVcNGRR53f13w

References

Amemiya, Karin. 2018. *Hiseiki, Tanshin, Arafo Josei* (Single Women in their Forties with Irregular Work). Tokyo: Kobunsha.

Ebihara, Tsuguo. 2012. *Joshi no Kyaria* (Women's Careers). Tokyo: Chikuma Shobo.

Esping-Andersen, Gosta. 1990. *The Three Worlds of Welfare Capitalism*. London: Polity Press.

Esping-Andersen, Gosta. 2009. *The Incomplete Revolutionn: Adapting to Women's New Roles*. London: Polity Press.

Fineman, Martha A. 1995. *The Neutered Mother, the Sexual Family and Other Twentieth Century Tragedies*. New York: Taylor and Francis Books Inc.

Finamen, Martha A. 2004. *The Autonomy Myth: A Theory of Dependency*. New York: The New Press.

Frazer, Nancy. 1993. "After the Family Wage: Gender Equality and the Welfare State." *Political Theory* 22 (4):591–618.

Hamaguchi, Keiichiro. 2015. *Hataraku Joshi no Unmei* (The Destiney of Working Women). Tokyo: Bungeishunjusha.

Hashimoto, Kenji. 2018. *Shin Nihon no Kaikyu Shakai* (A New Class Society of Japan). Tokyo: Kodansha.

Kawaguchi, Akira. 2008. *Jenda Keizai Kakusa* (Economical Gender Gap). Keiso Shobo.

Nakano, Madoka. 2014. *Ikukyu Sedai no Jiremmna* (A Dilemma of the Working Women with Childcare Leave). Tokyo: Kobunsha.

Okano, Yayo. 2012. *Feminizumu no Seijigaku* (A Poltics of Feminism). Tokyo: Misuzu Shobo.

Osawa, Mari. 1993. *Kigyou Chushin Shakai wo Koete* (Beyond Corporate Centered Society). Jiji Tsushinsha. 2020 New ed. Tokyo: Iwanami Publishers.

Ruddick, Sara. 1989. *Maternal Thinking: Toward a Politics of Peace*. New York: Columbia University Press.

Ueno, Chizuko. 1990. *Kafuchosei to Shihonsei* (Patriarchy and Capitalism). 2008 New ed. Tokyo: Iwanami Publishers.

Ueno, Chizuko. 2013. *Onna-tachi no Sabaibaru Sakusen* (A Women's Strategy for Survival). Tokyo: Bungeishunjusha.

Yamaguchi, Kazuo. 2017. *Hatarakikata No Danjo Fubyodo: Riron to Jissho Bunnseki* (Gender Inequality of Working Style: Theory and Evidence Analysis). Tokyo: Nihon Keizai Shinbunsha.

Yoshikawa, Toru. 2018. *Nihon no Bundan* (Japan on the Divide). Kobunsha.

Impact of Marxist feminism on Japanese women's movement: Focusing on the domestic labor debates

Kumiko Ida

ABSTRACT

The term Marxist feminism was introduced from the West and appeared in Japan after the 1980s. The representative theorist was Ueno Chizuko, who greatly contributed to the development of feminist theories in Japan, including Marxist feminism. It should be noted that this argument was not new in Japan, and in the 1970s, when the domestic labour theories began to be discussed in Western countries, there existed in Japan the original discussions by Takenaka Emiko, Iijima Aiko and others, which go back to the issue of socialist women, such as Yamakawa Kikue, before the Second World War. Of particular note was the 1960 housewife debate by Isono Fujiko and Mizuta Tamae, which had already pioneered Marxist feminism and most of the theorists in the 1970s succeeded the argument of the 1960s. Since the 1990s, the perspective of considering housework and childcare as labour has been reflected in social support for child and elderly care enacting the related laws. The change was accompanied by the women's labour movement and women's human rights issues such as the elimination of violence against women. It can be said that the recognition that 'housework is labour', formed by the domestic labour debate, as a whole, contributed to shake the patriarchal concept of labour and empowered the emergence of various movements concerning women that had been overlooked before.

Introduction

An interesting phenomenon related to the 1985 census questionnaire was captured by Ueno Chizuko (1995), well -known sociologist and feminist in Japan. A reader complained that he disagreed with the classification in the questionnaire of people who did only 'housework' as 'people who did not work at all' and asked, 'Isn't housework labor?' (Asahi Shinbun, 2.10.1985). Ueno suggests that the fact that it was a complaint from a 52-year-old man may indicate that the recognition that housework is labor was widely shared in Japanese society at that time. Five years before, in the 1980 census, this kind of complaint was not mentioned by major media, and Ueno found a change in the recognition of housework occurred in those five years between the censuses (Ueno 1995).

The 1980s were the time when Marxist feminist theory was introduced and discussed in Japan by feminists, including Ueno, one of the most famous feminist researchers. The trend surely influenced changes in the recognition of housework: previously there were widespread satirical references to the life of a housewife, such as "three meals and a nap included". As Ueno added, an increase of women working in the market, also prompted the change. However, needless to say, social recognition is not just a mirror of real conditions. Instead, it depends on reconceptualization to reveal a reality that has been overlooked before. In order to recognize that housework is labor, it is important that a person who engages in housework must be considered an independent person who makes a contribution to the economy. The debate over domestic work had been around for a long time, but changes in social recognition would not have occurred without the second-wave feminist movement speaking out for the individuality of women in households, with the slogan 'the personal is political'.

This paper aims to examine the impact of Marxist feminism, focusing on the debates on domestic labor, keeping in view the original debates developed in Japan before the arrival of the Western theories, and their effect on the issues tackled by women's movements.

Historical questions on housework: debate on housework and housewife in the 1960s

'Whether housework is labor or not?' is a historical question that has been repeatedly brought up for a long time. In Japan, this question was raised long before the 'arrival' of the term 'Marxist feminism'. In the first half of the 20th century, a prominent socialist activist, Yamakawa Kikue insists " After all women's work at home is nothing but unpaid labor." (Yamakawa 1918), and points out the roots of male dominance in the capitalist economy and patriarchy as a family system (Yamakawa 1923). Takenaka Emiko, pioneer in women's labor research and one of the leading Marxist feminists in Japan, evaluates Yamakawa's ideas as "the origin of Marxist feminism in Japan." (Takenaka 1991).

Subsequently, several controversies over 'housewives' developed during the period of high economic growth after the second world war[1]. Among them, the controversy on the value of housework, triggered by Isono Fujiko [2](1960), was almost a precursor to the domestic labor controversy in the 1970s in Western countries. Isono's article written from the viewpoint of a housewife, disagrees with the theory of Marxian economics, which defines housework as value-unproductive. She argued that housework is the labor that reproduces the husband's labor power commodity, and housewives cannot be convinced that their work does not produce any value. She made an inference that housework is not considered value-productive because housewives were not recognized as independent persons. Suppose that wives belonged to their husbands, it would be overlooked who had the burden to take care of husbands. Considering housework as not value-productive, she argued, means that housewives are not regarded as independent and equal to their husbands. However, the responses to Isono's question by Marxian economists were rather dogmatic. They 'taught' her with a condescending attitude the established theory of Marxian economics, that housework is not value-productive because it is considered as private work. At that time, Isono's question did not result in any change of the established theory of Marxian economics.

Looking back at this controversy later, 'at that time it was concluded that housewife labor did not create value within the framework of Marxism', says Mizuta Tamae[3] (Mizuta 1980), who participated to the controversy. Mizuta's paper, written as one of the responses to Isono, fully accepted the question raised by Isono, and pointed out, 'housewife labor includes labor for childbirth, childcare, and education, that creates the bearer of the future labor force, and a labor force of husbands and family members' (Mizuta 1960). She added that the low wages of young new employees are supported by the unpaid work of mothers and the society is supported by the unpaid work of housewives, and she insisted that the labor of housewives creates surplus value. She advocated the application of a "pension" system[4], specifically social benefits to remunerate unpaid work of housewives, insisting that unpaid and useful housewife labor should be socially rewarded (Mizuta 1960). This domestic labor debate, that predates the translation of Western feminist writings on the topic, took place in the early days of Japanese high-growth period, when drastic transformation in the industrial structure from primary industry to secondary and tertiary promoted migration to urban areas and an increase in nuclear families with full-time housewives. The argument that the work of housewife was value-productive was also criticized by the activists of the women's labor movement based on the socialist theory of women's emancipation, which presupposed that 'women must continue to work in the market to be equal to men', and was concerned about the danger of confining the role of women to domestic affairs. In the context of socialist movements, the housewife was considered a remnant of pre-modern "feudalism" from which women should be liberated . So these activists argued that if housework were considered economically valuable, it would be regarded as women's role to continue to do this work.

Isono's question and Mizuta's response to it are similar to the contribution to Western discussion by Mariarosa Dalla Costa and Selma James (1972), which triggered the domestic labor controversy that developed in the 1970s.

In this era in Japan, when the Marxist tradition was extremely strong, the theory that housework is a value-productive labor, did not develop further, and Marxist economists responded to Isono's humble question of "begging for teaching" in a top down way by teaching Engels' theory. However, the debate over domestic labor was taken up again in the 1970s after the advent of the second wave of feminism.

Domestic labor theories in Japan in the 1970s

Before the introduction of Western theories, various domestic labor theories had already appeared in Japan in the early 1970s, the same period as in the West. Since the advent of second-wave feminism, the momentum for the feminist movement to explain the inferior status of women in capitalist society and to pave the way for its transformation has also been sustained in Japan. Many of the bearers of second-wave feminism were participants in the New Left radicalism and were influenced by the movement of students in the late 1960s. The articles of feminist activists at the time show that they felt strongly the necessity to theorize the relationship between capitalism and sexism before the term 'Marxist feminism' arrived. Mizuta's description of the 1970s reminds us of the momentum at that time as follows

> Until the 1960s, Marxism was the most influential guideline in the field of women's issues in Japan. However, the situation changed when the Women's Liberation Movement ("Uhman Ribu" in Japanese) was introduced in the 1970s. The movement, which aimed to review established values with the eyes of women, also targeted Marxism. This movement, based on the New Left, which criticized the traditional Left movement, was born of the disappointment that the New Left also discriminates against women. So it was inevitable to re-examine the Marxism that had provided the theoretical support of the Left and New Left… The criticism of Marxism by women's liberation movement touches the basics of Marxism. While it may be natural for Marxists to adhere to the traditional Marxist dogma, its defensive stance seems to be too dependent on claims to Marxist authority, and it seems hard to say that it was a convincing enough answer to criticism (Mizuta 1980).

Supporting the claims of the Women's Liberation Movement that appeared in the 1970s, Mizuta argues, 'Sexism and the conflict of sexes is an issue of different dimensions, although not unrelated to class discrimination and class struggle' (Mizuta 1980). However, the Marxist response was dogmatic and authoritarian, criticizing feminist theories for not following Engels' teachings and lacking a class perspective, and, excessively emphasizing the difference of the sexes and ignoring the struggle of the working class. Moreover, the Marxists insisted that the proletariat has no private property and thus lacks a basis for sexism; therefore, it was wrong to apply to the family of the proletariat the 'analysis of a patriarchal family' (Mizuta 1980). Despite the advent of the New Left movement, the response from Marxism was almost unchanged from the time of the housewife controversy in the 1960s.

Tanaka Mitsu, the flag bearer of the Uhman-Ribu (Women's Liberation) movement, criticized Marxist theory for making invisible the reality in front of us. The beginning of Tanaka's famous essay of revolutionary passion, entitled 'Even Small Sparks Burn the Wilderness', begins with a provocation to the New Left activists.

> 'Fogy revolutionists' say that there is no viewpoint of class in the perspective of 'woman'. What is the class? According to Marxist doctrine, it might be justified to say 'proletariat is the only revolutionary subject', but it's time to say goodbye to chanting a slogan that means almost nothing (Tanaka 1971).

Tanaka Mitsu is a famous feminist of Uhman-Ribu (Women's Liberation Movement), and a founder of a significant radical feminist group in Japan, 'Guruhp Tatakau Onna (Group of Fighting Women)'. She discusses domestic work in this essay with the question, 'Why did the old wife go to the river to do the washing?'[5] Tanaka suggests that the domestic role of women is a result of sexual subordination to men. Sexuality and social reproduction are discussed here as labor:

> A value system with reproduction at the top … It's this value system, which appears wrapped in the comfortable words 'marriage is the happiness of a woman' that puts a woman as a labour power commodity into low wage work and makes her an unpaid domestic worker… By being forced to do household chores, the woman is forced into the position of a maid with a house, and diligently makes cheap purchases to cover low wages and indirectly serve the profits of capitalists. In addition, she plays the role of a slave trader who refreshes a man who has been worn out by competition to survive and sends him back to the market as a labour power commodity (Tanaka 1971).

Another significant group of Japanese second-wave feminism was 'Shinryaku = Sabetu to Tatakau Ajia Fujin Kaigi (Conference of Asian Women Fighting Against Discrimination as Invasion)'. Japanese second-wave feminism is said to have been started by" Ribu Gasshuku", the Women's Liberation Weekend Camp held in August of 1971, but the Conference of Asian Women Fighting Against Discrimination as Invasion was held in August 1970, a year before the Camp and prior to the formation of Tanaka's 'Guruhp Tatakau Onna (Group of Fighting Woman)' in October 1970. The Asian Women's Conference functioned as a place to prepare for the formation of 'Group of Fighting Woman' (Kano 2011).

'Shinryaku = Sabetu to Tatakau Ajia Fujin Kaigi' (Conference of Asian Women Fighting Against Discrimination as Invasion)continued to be active for 10 years after the first conference. Iijima Aiko, who was consistently at the center of the activities of Conference of Asian Women, had been involved in the socialist labor movement for many years and was formed intellectually as a materialist, proposed to reconsider sexual discrimination as a matter of exploitation rather than of ideological consciousness. Based on the understanding of wages as the cost of social reproduction, she said that housework, including childcare work, is nothing but the process of reproduction and regeneration of the social labor power. Iijima discusses the main issues of second wave feminism, sexuality and reproduction, from the viewpoint of labor. Iijima says, "Women sell their sexuality to men through marriage." and "Housework and childcare labor socially forced on housewives is a function associated with the sexuality of the wife as a commodity". She disagrees with the housework controversy in the 1960s in which housework was considered as labor in general. According to her, housework is associated with the sexuality of the wife possessed by her husband as a commodity.

This issue of "sexuality as labor", discussed in the movement early in the 1970s, disappeared as the domestic labor was defined academically as part of the field of economics, and the issue of sexuality became tackled as a problem of the violence against women and an issue of human rights of women (Ida 2019).

At the same time, Takenaka Emiko, a Marxian labor economist and a pioneer in women's labor research proposed a theory that incorporates domestic work in the reproduction and commercialization of labor power (Takenaka 1972).

While Tanaka and Iijima discussed domestic work as activists from the perspective of the women's liberation movement, Takenaka replied as an economist by conceptualizing the process of the reproduction of the labor power as part of the capitalist mode of production, discussing how patriarchy works in the capitalist system. Tanaka (1971) and Iijima (1972) drew on their passion as activists to explain the connection between the unpaid work of housewives and the low-wage labor of female workers in the labor market. Takenaka discussed the same issue from the perspective of labor economics research based on Marxian economics. The question raised by Isono in the 1960s, disregarded by Marxian economists, was finally picked up by Takenaka in the field of Marxian labor economics, even if it remained in a marginal position. This was possible only because Takenaka was a rare female labor researcher who fully accepted the new issues raised by the women's liberation movement, which was the target of intense ridicule and was rejected by many female researchers and social activists. At the beginning of her career, Takenaka adopted the issue of women's labor as a lifelong research topic, which remained marginal in the field of labor economics at that time. The decision was based on her experience as a researcher with the family burden of housework and childcare and a deep doubt about why women's housework was not a subject of economics. Takenaka took up Isono's articles in the housewife controversy as a "housework labor theory of value" and states that it demands in particular wages for housework. She gives a view that women must have been dissatisfied at the replies of Marxist economists and such dissatisfaction was one of the driving forces behind the emergence of Uhman Ribu movement (Takenaka 1974). As mentioned above, in the housewife controversy most of the socialist women's labor movement activists opposed to Isono's view that the value of housework should be recognized, because they insisted that to achieve gender equality, all the women should engage in productive labor in the labor market rather than valuing housework. Uhman Ribu movement was promoted by different women from the conventional women's labor movement and the position of the housewife was one of the main subjects because Uhman Ribu movement focused on the "private" sphere such as family, sexuality and reproduction.

The work of Tanaka and Iijima had a wide political impact, but Takenaka's work was accepted in particular by activists and students who participated to the left and new left movements. Her theory on the inferior position of women in the capitalist system empowered the generation of students and activist women, that was plagued by the attacks of left-wing men that "feminism has no class perspective." Although there were conflicts in the women's movements due to the different positions of political parties such as Socialist and Communists, Takenaka's books were widely read across parties[6].

However, while Takenaka fully understood and evaluated the significance of the Women's Liberation movement, which makes sexuality an important issue, unlike Tanaka and Iijima, she herself did not make sexuality an issue in her theorizing about labor. In that respect, this was similar to Western Marxist feminism in the domestic labor controversy. Perhaps discussing sexuality from the perspective of labor was unexpected in the frame of economics, and I think it is an issue to be discussed again today (Ida 2019).

The arrival of the Western Marxist feminism in Japan and the contribution of Ueno Chizuko

It was around 1980 that Western Marxist feminist theory became known in Japan. The Women's Liberation movement was initially thoroughly ridiculed and rejected not only by the conservatives but also by the leftists, but after the UN World Conference on Women held in 1975 and the new development of women's movements triggered by it, the direction of the wind in Japanese society was changing a little. Mizuta serialized an introduction to Western Marxist feminism, including the theory of domestic labor, in "Mirai", free publicity brochure of the publisher Miraisha[7]. The series was entitled "The Perspective of Women's Liberation." In this series, Mizuta systematically took up major articles, including that by Mariarosa Dalla Costa (1972), putting forward the demand of wages for housework[8]. In the field of economics, Kuba Yoshiko (1979) and Takenaka (1980) had already begun to introduce major papers on the domestic labor controversy, but this series was the first comprehensive introduction to the theories on the relationship of Marxism and feminism. However, it was serialized in a limited media such as the publicity brochure of a publisher, and it was an unfinished serialization that was not resumed after interruption, and its readership seems to have been limited.

1980 was also the year when the Japanese translation of the English version of Dalla Costa (1972) was published. Takenobu Mieko, an active journalist specializing in labor issues, was the representative of the group of translators, Group 7221, that carried out the translation. Takenobu maintains a strong interest in domestic work in her activities; she read Takenaka (1972) and experienced "scales falling from her eyes."

However, it is clear that Marxist feminism in Japan has become widely known due to the success of Ueno Chizuko. Marxist feminism attracted a great deal of attention among feminists in Japan in the 1980s through the vigorous talks and publications of Ueno. The booklet "*Shihonsei to Kajiroudou*[Capitalism and Housework]" (1985) containing Ueno's lecture was widely read as an introductory book. And Ueno led not only Marxist feminism but feminist theories in general in Japan, and greatly enhanced the presence of feminism in both academic circles and social movements. Ueno, who has been an outstanding controversialist made second wave feminism widely known to society, calling her role that of an "interpreter".

Ueno was also one of the feminists who took up the question of the housewife controversies, and was strongly aware of its importance. The editing by Ueno of two volumes (1982) collecting of the main articles, *Shufuronsou wo Yomu* [*Reading the Housewife Controversies*] is a precious effort that greatly contributed to the subsequent development of feminism and gender studies in Japan. Soon after, in 1984 Ueno supervised the translation of a collection of major articles of the domestic labor controversy in the UK, *Feminism and Materialism* edited by A Kuhn and A. Volpe (1978). In the commentary introducing this translation, Ueno defined Marxist feminism as an integration of socialist women's emancipation theory, a theory based primarily on class, and radical feminism, a theory based exclusively on sexism. Ueno argued that Marxist feminism stipulates that capital and patriarchy are mutually independent variables, and analyses both market domination and sexual domination to understand both as mutually complementary. And she continues, following Natalie Sokoloff (1980), translated in 1987, the relationship between capitalism and patriarchy is defined as "dialectical", and the relationship between the two is not just a collaborative relationship, but includes contradictions and conflicts.

In 1986, two further works on the domestic labor debate were translated. One was the collection of articles written by Mariarosa Dalla Costa (1986) in the 1970s, *Kajiroudou ni Chingin wo: Feminizumu no Aratana Tenbou* (*Wages for Housework: New Perspective of Feminism*), and the other Barbara Duden and Claudia Von Werlhof's collection, *Kajiroudou to Shihonnshugi* (*Housework and Capitalism*). The domestic labor theories attracted widespread interest, together with the introduction of the concept of 'shadow work' by Ivan Illich's book with the same title (1982).

These discussions by Italian and German feminists were defined by Sokoloff as a previous stage of Marxist feminist theories. They discussed the structure in which family and community, considered 'outside' the area of the market, continue to be heavily exploited by the capitalist system. They consider women's subordination as a base of capitalism, different from the categorization of patriarchy as independent from capitalism, characteristic of the Marxist feminist theory of Ueno.

Controversy on Marxist feminism

Various criticisms have emerged of Ueno's Marxist feminism. Ueno responded to criticism in the culmination of her work on Marxist feminism, *Kafuchosei to Shihonsei* (*Patriarchy and Capitalism*) (1990). According to her, the criticism was less from feminists and more from Marxists. Ueno considers this quantitative imbalance as characteristic of a situation in which "feminists have little interest in Marxism, and Marxists perceived my Marxist feminism as some kind of challenge or bias" (Ueno 1990: 130). However, there was little reaction from "male Marxists", probably indifferent to feminism, and most of the criticisms were by "female Marxists and some young male researchers who were baptized in feminism", and "It was from the standpoint of defending the wholeness of Marxist theory," (Ueno 1990: 141–142). "To be a Marxist feminist, one must first recognize the premise of radical feminism, the concept of 'patriarchy', separately from capitalism" (ibid .: 134–135). We will focus on the criticism by Takenaka, considered by Ueno as a "female Marxist", because it is a representative view in this controversy.

Takenaka did not agree with Ueno's Marxist feminism based on so-called "dualism" that regards patriarchy and capitalism as independent each other. Takenaka proposed to reconstruct the gender blind concept of production as well as the 'narrow' concept of economics of classic Marxism through radical criticism of Marxian economics because capitalism itself includes gender hierarchy (Takenaka 1989). Furthermore, focusing on the theory of Veronica Beechey based on the theory of labor process and social reproduction (Beechey 1987), Takenaka criticized dualism because 'it accepts the Marxian sex-blind analysis of the production relations and connects it with another concept, patriarchy, something totally different… It tends to point an accusing finger mainly to patriarchy overlooking capitalism' (Takenaka 1989).

In summary, Takenaka argued that "dualism" cannot analyze the labor market and labor process from the perspective of gender. The dual theory regards the family and the state as "outside" of the market and controlled by the patriarchal system, independent from capitalism. However, in practice the market strongly depends on these "outside institutions", family and the state, but this dependence is not sufficiently brought into focus in "dualism".

After this debate on Marxist feminism there seems to have arisen a certain distance between the interdisciplinary associations of women's studies and women's labor economics, the main fields of the Marxist feminist debate in the 1980s.

Research in women's labor economics has been marginalized, and many women engaging in this field had difficulty to obtain research positions in academia. This was not just a problem of labor economics, but a common experience in many disciplines. Many researchers engaged in women's and gender studies while working in existing disciplines[9]. The Women's Studies Associations were launched one after another in the late 1970s and have worked as interdisciplinary and gathering places for researchers and activists to try to offset marginalization. In the 1980s, several seminars on Marxist feminism were held by the Women's Studies Society of Japan, where Takenaka, Kuba, and Ueno participated as speakers and discussed together. Takenaka (1984) is a lecture text of her conference held by the Women's Studies Society of Japan. However, since the 1990s, researchers in women's labor economics have been able to develop their activities in conventional academic societies (such as the Social Policy Society), and their contact with the Women's Studies Associations has diminished. It must be an outcome of the effort of the feminist researchers that traditional academic organizations have come to accept women's perspective. But perhaps as a result of it, the participation of economists in the interdisciplinary exchange on women's and gender studies seems to have been deactivated.

At the 2009 symposium on women's poverty held by the Women's Studies Association of Japan, it was said that women's studies had paid little attention to the problem of labor and poverty issues. A similar remark was expressed by a leader of the women's labor movement affirming that feminism has not addressed labor and poverty issues.[10] It was clearly a misunderstanding because feminist studies have addressed these issues and have engaged with some important practical issues relating to women's labor, poverty, and care problems. To give an example, Ueno (2011) has tackled elderly care issues. Moreover she wrote a trial opinion for one of the Sumitomo wage discrimination trials. However, the misunderstanding may have come from a certain distance between the "mainstream" women's studies, one of the leading researchers of which was Ueno, and the women's labor studies promoted by Takenaka, Kuba etc. Anyway it should be noted that Marxist feminism as a whole, contributed to focus on the recognition of women's work, unpaid and paid. The recognition of work is based on the recognition of the independent personhood of the person who engages in it, as Isono insisted in the housewife controversy in the 1960s. The recognition of the economic importance of unpaid work has been accompanied by the recognition of the economic importance of the paid and underpaid labor of women, for long considered as unskilled and providing merely supplementary income and overlooked by the existing trade unions. A remarkable development of new women's labor movements appeared since the late 1980s and 1990s, such as the foundation of women's labor unions and the struggles organized by women with little support of the existing trade unions. In Japan, several women's labor unions were formed in the late 1980s and 1990s. The existing trade unions had not fully addressed the issue of women's labor, and some had even been hostile. For example, the plaintiff Yakabi in the Pay Equity Trial suffered severe harassment from the existing trade union and was isolated at work (Yakabi 2007). She is a founding member of the first women's labor union in Japan, "Onna Roudou Kumiai Kansai (Women's Labour Union in Kansai)", which was formed in Osaka in 1988. In addition, the Sumitomo Trials could get little cooperation from the trade unions of the companies which denied discrimination and refused to show the specific data on actual wages (Miyaji and Working Women's Network 2005).

The impact of domestic labor theories on women's labor movement and social policy in Japan

The dramatic decline in the birth rate at the end of the 1980s and the rapid progress of ageing forced a fairly fundamental shift in social policy in the 1990s, and the policy response to childbirth, childcare and elderly care began in earnest. Frankly, these are not the direct consequences of the women's movement. However, it can be assumed that the rapid decline in birth rate, all beyond expectation, was the result of women's refusal to any longer bear the increasingly heavy family burden on women, and their wish to become much more autonomous and independent. As mentioned at earlier in this article, it was exactly in the 1980s when the recognition that 'housework is labor' became prevalent.

In 1991, the Childcare Leave Law was enacted with unusual rapidity for all employees, including the private sector and male workers[11]. In 1995, elderly care was added to the Leave. The Elderly Care Insurance Law[12] was enacted in 1997. These changes show that child and elderly care, which was considered natural to be performed privately by housewives or other female members of the family, changed significantly from leaving this to the family to providing social support. It means that housework performed mainly by women is definitely recognized as labor. All the social support policies realized in the 1990s are based on this change in the concept of labor.

The recognition that "housework is labor" and "working women bear a double burden" has succeeded in shaking up the traditional concept of labor standardized on the lives of male heads of household. This also contributed directly and indirectly to the improved recognition of women's paid labor in the labor market.

In Japan, the 1990s were a time when the women's labor movement achieved epoch-making results, while the traditional male-centered labor movement declined. The trade union organization rate has gradually declined since the 1980s, dropping to 16.7% in 2019. The main factor is the increase in non-regular workers. The Japanese labor unions are centered on male regular employees and most non-regular workers are women. Part-time and temporary work has been regarded as suitable work styles for women who have a family responsibility and a husband as breadwinner. Clerical jobs such as the job of the plaintiffs in the Sumitomo Tribunal have been regarded as auxiliary work for women, even if they are full-time employees, and have been kept at low wages without being properly evaluated. The result is that the women's labor movement has challenged this and achieved breakthrough results even as the traditional male-centered labor movement has retreated significantly. Several legal cases on wage discrimination based on gender or employment status were brought to court, and all of them were concluded in favor of the plaintiffs. The Sumitomo cases[13] and that of Kyogas[14] were on gender wage discrimination. The Maruko Alarm case[15] was on wage discrimination based on employment status, but all the plaintiffs were women also in this case. The supporters of Sumitomo and Kyogas cases were voluntary groups of women because the trade unions in these companies didn't cooperate with the plaintiffs. Only the case of Maruko was tackled by the trade union.

In the Kyogas case, the pay equity method and a written opinion on job evaluation based on the pay equity method were adopted. Job evaluation was also adopted in another gender wage discrimination case, that of the trading company Kanematsu, which also led to a favorable judgment in 2009.

These cases were about gender discrimination in the wage for paid work, but when unpaid housework is overlooked, paid work of women is also undervalued because it is supposed that women don't have to be paid sufficiently because they are dependents of male heads of households and their primary contribution is housework. The controversy on the economic status of housework, which prompted a recognition that housework is an economic contribution, and that housewives should be treated as persons in their own right, triggered changes in the recognition also of women's right to dignified and equal conditions of paid labor.

Yakabi Fumiko, the plaintiff of the Kyogas case, subsequently campaigned to promote job evaluation and pay equity, with the aim of improving low wages, especially in care work. Yakabi argues that the low wages for women's jobs were the result of the undervaluation of unpaid domestic work because many women's jobs, such as care work, are regarded as an extension of unpaid domestic work. She advocates that the method of job evaluation based on the theory of pay equity can be beneficial to the elimination of wage discrimination.[16]

Domestic labor theories also shed light on the ideological function of 'love', which especially influenced the theory of care labor. Kasuga Kisuyo, in her article on elderly care labor, cited the theory of Giovanna Franca Dalla Costa (1978) translated in 1991, and discussed the way in which the invocation of 'love' obscures labor (Kasuga 2001). Domestic labor theories also contributed to raising the issue of domestic violence against women as a serious social problem from the perspective of exploitation of unpaid labor. In fact, the first survey on domestic violence carried out by feminist activists in 1992 showed that dissatisfaction with housework can often trigger domestic violence (Otto/Koibito kara no Bouryoku Chosa Kenkyukai [Research Group on Violence by Husband/Boyfriend] 1998).

Conclusion

This paper surveyed the development of Marxist feminism in Japan from the housewife controversy in the 1960s to the second wave feminist period in the 1970s, and the 1980s with the arrival of Western theories. It argued that the overturning of the male-centered concept of labor and workers became one of the forces that promoted the changes in social policy since the 1990s and some of the outcomes of the women's labor movement. Various debates have continued since the 1990s, and self-criticisms of Marxist feminism suggest specific case studies should be tackled (Kimoto 2000). The momentum for a new development of a feminist theory as a criticism of capitalism is rising again today.

As was the case with Marxist feminism in the second wave of feminism, the theory emerges from within the movement at the request of the movement, not the other way around. But theory can change recognitions and change society. It can be said that domestic labor theory has succeeded in promoting changes in the standard male-centered concept of labor and worker, empowering women's movements, and achieving some practical results.

Notes

1. The main articles contributing to the housewife controversies were collected and edited by Ueno in two volumes in 1982, which is one of her great academic contributions.
2. Isono Fujiko is the author of "Family System" (1958), co-authored with Isono Seiichi, a civil law scholar. She is specialized in Mongolian studies.
3. Mizuta Tamae researches social thought and specializes in the history of modern feminist thoughts in Europe.
4. Japanese current pension system was founded in 1961, and in 1960 when Mizuta wrote this article there existed only social benefits system for elderlies, disabled and single mothers. So the "pension" system proposed by Mizuta is a social benefit.
5. It is a passage of Japanese popular folk tale, 'Momotaro'.
6. One of the important cases of the political conflicts was the division of Fujin Minshu Kurabu (Women's Democratic Club), founded in 1946, soon after the end of the Second World War. It divided in 1970 into two sections, one socialist group (the mainstream), and the other communist. Recently this type of political conflict seems to be fading out at least in the field of women's movements.
7. Japanese publishers produce publicity brochures to introduce and contextualize new publications. Usually one can take them for free at the cash counter of bookstores. The publicity brochures are of high quality and serve as the 'signature' of a publisher.
8. I read this series right before departing to study in Italy in 1980 and there searched for a domestic labour movement, but by this time the movement had disappeared without a trace.
9. Universities with women's studies courses are extremely limited, and they are certainly concentrated in women's universities.
10. The remark was made by Ito Midori, one of the founders of Women's labour union Tokyo in the interview of Shukan Kin-youbi, a weekly magazine, in 2008.
11. A parental leave until the child is one year old, and initially without income security that gradually increased to over 50%. Elderly care leave can be taken up to 93 days.
12. The main body of the system is the municipalities that provide the necessary long-term care services funded with insurance premiums and taxes. The service of housework for the elderly is included and paid.

13. Gender wage discrimination cases brought in 1995 by nine plaintiffs against Sumitomo Electric Industries, Sumitomo Chemical, and Sumitomo Metal, and all the cases finished with the judgement in favour of the plaintiffs betweem 2004 and 2006.
14. Gender wage discrimination in different jobs in Kyogas, a gas company in Kyoto, was brought to court with a favourable judgment in 2001.
15. Wage discrimination against part-time workers engaged in the same job as full-time employees in Maruko Keihouki (Maruko Alarm Company) in Nagano. The judgment was that more than 20% of the difference of the wages was considered contrary to public order and standards of decency.
16. Yakabi organised the Pay Equity Consulting Office and published educational tools such as booklets and DVDs.

References

Dalla Costa, Giovanna Franca. 1978. *Un lavoro d'amore: La violenza fisica componente essenziale del "trattamento" maschile nei confronti delle donne. Edizioni delle donne.* Translated by Kumiko Ida. 1991. *Ai no Roudou* [Labour of Love]. Tokyo: Inpakuto-shuppankai.

Dalla Costa, Mariarosa. 1986. *Kajiroudou ni Chingin wo: Feminizumu No Aratana Tenkai* [Wages for Housework: New Stage of Feminism]. Translated by Kumiko Ida and Kimio Ito. Tokyo: Inpakuto-Shuppankai.

Dalla Costa, Mariarosa, and Selma James. 1972. "The Power of Women and the Subversion of the Community." In *Capitalism: The Family and Personal Life*, edited by Eli Zaretsky. Pluto Press. Translated by Groupe 7221. 1980. *Shihonshugi, Kazoku, Kojinseikatsu* [Capitalism: the Family and Personal Life]. Tokyo: Aki-shobo: 157–211.

Duden, Barbara, and Claudia Von Werlhov. 1986. *Kajiroudou to Shihonshugi* [Domestic Labour and Capitalism]. Translated by Masato Maruyama. Tokyo: Iwanami-shoten.

Ida, Kumiko. 2019. *Roudou tositeno sekushuariti* [Sexuality as Labour] Joseigaku-kenkyu, No.26. Center for Women's Studies of Osaka Prefecture University: 1–18.

Iijima, Aiko. 1972. "*Onna ni totte Sakushu towa Nanika*". [The Meaning of Exploitation for Women]. In *Shinryaku = Sabetsu no Kanata e* [Over the Discrimination as Invasion], edited by Aiko Iijima, 201–217. Tokyo: Inpakuto Shuppankai.

Illich, Ivan. 1982. *Shadow Work. Marion Boyars.* Translated by Yoshiro Tamanoi, et al. *Shado Wahku* [Shadow *Work*]. Tokyo: Iwanami-shoten.

Isono, Fujiko. 1960. "*Fujinkaihouron no Konmei*" [Turmoil of the Theory of Women's Liberation]." In *Shufuronso wo Yomu* [Reading Controversies on Housewife], edited by Chizuko Ueno. 1982: 2–22. Tokyo: Keiso-shobo.

Ito, Midori. 2008. "*Ikari wo Chikara ni Tenkan suru.*" [Turn Anger into Power]. *Shukan Kin'yobi No* 722:24–26.

Kano, Mikiyo. 2011. "*Shinryaku = Sabetsu to Tatakau Ajia Fujin Kaigi to Dainiha Feminizumu* [Asian Women's Conference to Fight Discrimination as Invasion and the second wave feminism]." *Joseigaku-kenkyu*, 18:149–165. Center for Women's Studies of Osaka Prefecture University.

Kasuga, Kisuyo. 2001. *Kaigo-mondai no Shakaigaku* [Sociology of Elderly Care Issue]. Tokyo: Iwanami-shoten.

Kimoto, Kimiko. 2000. *Roudou to jenda* [Labour and Gender]. Ohara-shakaimondaiken-kyujo-zasshi no.500: 2000–7. 2–16.

Kuba, Yoshiko. 1979. *Kajiroudou to Seisan Yousiki* [Domestic Labour and the Mode of Production]." *Keizai-hyouron* 28-03:102–113.

Kuba, Yoshiko. 1987. "*Marukusushugi Feminizumu no kadai* [Issues of Marxist Feminism]". In *Onna no Me de Miru* [From the Viewpoint of Women], edited by Association for Women's Studies, 200–232. Tokyo: Keiso-shobo.

Kuhn, Annette, and AnnMarie Wolpe. eds. 1978. *Feminism and Materialism: Women and Modes of Production.* Routledge. Translated by Chizuko Ueno et al. 1984. *Marukusushugifeminizumu no Chousen* [Challenge of Marxist Feminism]. Tokyo: Keiso-shobo.

Miyaji, Mitsuko & Working Women's Network. eds. 2005. *"Kojoryozoku" ni Makenakatta Onnatachi* [Women Who did not Lose to" Public Order and Morals"]. Tokyo: Akashi-shoten.

Mizuta, Tamae. 1960. "*Shufuroudou no Nedan* [The Price of Housewife's Labour]." In *Shufuronso wo Yomu* [Reading Controversies on Housewife], *II.* Edited by Chizuko Ueno, 23–43. Tokyo: Keiso-shobo.

Mizuta, Tamae. 1980. "Josei-Kaiho no Shiten - Feminism and Marxism" 1 ~ 7, *Mirai* no. 165 ~ 171. Mirai-sha.

Otto/Koibito kara no Bouryoku Chosa Kenkyukai [Research Group on violence by husband/boyfriend]. 1998. *Domesutikku Vaiorensu: Otto/Koibito karano Bouryoku wo Nakusutameni* [to Stop Domestic Violence by Husband/Boyfriend]. Tokyo: Yuhikaku.

Sokoloff, Natalie J. 1980. *Between money and love: Dialectics of Women, Work and the Family.* Praeger Publishers Inc. Translated by Ehara Yumiko, et al. 1987. Okane to Aijo no Aida. Tokyo: Keiso-shobo.

Takenaka, Emiko. 1972. "*Fujin Kaihou no Konnnichiteki Kadai.*" In *Takenaka Emiko Chosaku-shu* [Collection of the works of Takenaka Emiko] vol. VII, edited by Emiko Takenaka, 17–66. Tokyo: Akashi-shoten.

Takenaka, Emiko. 1974. "joseimondai to Watakusi" [Women's Issues and i]. In *Takenaka Emiko Chosaku-shu* [Collection of the works of Takenaka Emiko] vol. VII, edited by Emiko Takenaka, 67–104. Tokyo: Akashi-shoten.

Takenaka, Emiko. 1980. "*Roudouryoku Saiseisan no Seikaku to Kajiroudou*" [The Nature of the Reproduction of Labor Force and Domestic Labor]. *Keizaigaku-Zasshi* 81-01:49–71.

Takenaka, Emiko. 1984. "Shihonshugi to Kajiroudou – Sono Kankeisei" [The Relationship between Capitalism and Domestic Labor]. In *Takenaka Emiko Chosaku-shu* [Collection of the works of Takenaka Emiko] vol. VI, edited by Emiko Takenaka, 17–51. Tokyo: Akashi-shoten.

Takenaka, Emiko. 1989. "*1980 nendai no Marukusushugi Feminizumu ni tsuite.*" [On the Marxist Feminism in the 1980s]. In *Takenaka Emiko* Chosaku-shu *[Collection of the works of Takenaka Emiko]* vol. VII, edited by Emiko Takenaka, 67–104. Tokyo: Akashi-shoten.

Tanaka, Mitsu. 1971. "*Chiisana Hibana mo Kouya wo Yakitsukusu*" [Even Small Sparks Burn the Wilderness], *Kouzou* no. 101: 82–97. Tokyo: Keizaikozo-sha.

Takenaka, Emiko. 1991. "Nihon niokeru Marukusushugi Feminizumu no genryu" [Origine of Marxist Feminism in Japan]. In *Nihon Fujinmondaikonwakai Kaihou.* No. 51.

Ueno, Chizuko (ed.). 1982. *Shufuronso wo Yomu* [Reading Controversies on Housewife], I, II. Tokyo: Keiso-shobo.

Ueno, Chizuko. 1985. *Shihonsei to Kajiroudou* [Capitalism and Domestic Labour]. Tokyo: Kaimeisha.

Ueno, Chizuko. 1990. *Kafuchousei to Shihonsei* [Patriarchy and Capitalism]. Tokyo: Iwanami-shoten.

Ueno, Chizuko. 1995. “Roudou” Gainen no Jenda ka [Gendering of the concept of “Labor”]. In *Sai no Seijigaku* [Politics on Difference], edited by Chizuko Ueno. Tokyo: Iwanami-shoten.

Ueno, Chizuko. 2011. *Kea no Shakaigaku* [Sociology of Care]. Tokyo: Ota-shuppan.

Yakabi, Fumiko. 2007. *Nametara akan Onna no Roudou* [Don’t Make Light of Women’s Labour]. Tokyo: Akashi-shoten.

Yamakawa, Kikue. 1918. “Dansei Yuetsu no Rekishiteki Tenkai” [Historical Development of Male Superiority]. In *Yamakawa Kikue Shu* [Collection of the works of Yamakawa Kikue], vol. 1. 2011. Tokyo: Iwanami-Shoten.

Yamakawa, Kikue. 1923. *Bosei Hogo to Keizaiteki Dokuritsu* [Maternity protection and economic independence]. In *Yamakawa Kikue Shu* [Collection of the works of Yamakawa Kikue] vol. 1. Tokyo: Iwanami-Shoten.

Gender equality, paid and unpaid care and domestic work: Disadvantages of state-supported marketization of care and domestic work

Sumika Yamane

ABSTRACT
Gender inequality, caused by the unequal distribution of unpaid care and domestic work between genders, has been a major feminist issue for a long time. This article demonstrates that so-called gender equality policies, which aim to reduce the burden of women's unpaid care and domestic work through the state-supported marketization of these services, create a vulnerable group of under-paid care and domestic workers. Such policies widen income gap between women who can purchase these services and those who cannot. I will propose feminist initiatives for gender equality that address these problems

Introduction

Social reproduction of labor is at the core of feminist concerns for gender equality. Since equality in the labor market cannot be achieved as long as unpaid care and domestic work in households is mainly shouldered by women, feminists have elaborated a framework to recognize, reduce, and redistribute this unpaid work done by women (Elson 2017).

Redistribution, in the sense used by Elson (2017), requires men to do more unpaid care and domestic work. Although the number of hours spent by men on this work has gradually increased over the years, this approach to realizing gender equality in the allocation of unpaid work has recorded slow progress. However, as Elson (2017) notes, the amount of unpaid care and domestic work that has to be done by women for their households has been reduced globally in the last 30 years by public provision of infrastructure to provide services such as water, sanitation, energy and public transport, and by public provision of health, education, and care services delivered by public employees. More recently, in a trend that is not discussed by Elson (2017) some governments have supported, through tax allowances and/or subsidies, the marketization of care and domestic work that takes place within households. Such work is largely performed by women who are employed by households or by agencies that are paid by the government but are not part of the public sector. Policies to support the marketization of care and domestic work are often described as gender equality policies, but as this article argues, they ignore inequalities between women.

Some feminist scholars have focused on global inequalities, social reproduction, and "care-chains" (Ehrenreich and Hochschild 2003); their view is that the gender division of work is constructed not only by gender differences, but also by the intersection of differences in social class and ethnicity. The International Labor Organization (ILO) estimates the number of paid domestic workers to be 53–100 million in developing and developed countries (ILO 2011a). Most domestic workers are underpaid; their work is considered unskilled and low productivity, and until recently most have been engaged in informal work that is not regulated by labor laws. The adoption of the ILO Domestic Workers Convention No. 189, which aims to promote decent working conditions for domestic workers and formalize their work, has had a crucial impact on recognition of domestic workers (ILO 2011a). Domestic workers often provide care services as well as doing housework.

Reducing the burden of unpaid work and securing favorable working conditions for paid domestic workers are both crucial issues for gender equality. However, the underpayment of domestic work and inequality between women who employ paid domestic workers and women who are paid domestic workers has taken a back seat in the discussion on gender equality policies. This study critically reviews scholarly feminist discussions on unpaid care and domestic work and gender equality. First, I will discuss strategies for the valuation of unpaid and paid care and domestic work. Second, I will focus on the effects of state-supported marketization of care and domestic work on gender and class inequalities. The marketization of care and domestic work, often linked to using of migrant labor, has become a major part of policies in several developed countries over the past 30 years, including both "familialistic states" like those in Asia and "gender-equal states" like Sweden. Sweden has encouraged the employment by households of migrant workers for unskilled, non-regular domestic work by making the purchase of domestic services a tax-deductible expense. Japan has adopted a different strategy, providing public funding for care services to be delivered in households by workers employed by external agencies. These are both examples of state-supported marketization. Finally, I will propose a domestic work policy to bridge the income gap between women and improve the working conditions of domestic workers and care workers.

In the following sections, for brevity, I frequently use the term "unpaid work" to refer to work performed by family members (mainly women), including care work (for the children and frail family members) and domestic work (shopping, cooking, or washing). People who are paid to do these kinds of work in households are referred to in various ways in the literature. A person is usually considered to be a "domestic worker," when the worker is paid directly or indirectly by the household (though their work often includes care work as well as domestic work). A person is usually considered to be a "care worker," when the worker is paid directly or indirectly by the state (though if they are providing services within a household, their work may include domestic work as well as care work). I will use both terms, depending on the context, the relevant literature, and the examples under discussion.

Understanding the value of unpaid care and domestic work

The volume and value of unpaid care and domestic work

Based on the feminist thought that housework is labor that contributes to capitalism by enabling the reproduction of the existing workers and development of children as prospective workers (Barrett 1980; Dalla Costa and James 1972), the measurement of the volume and value of unpaid work began to be considered a central aspect of gender equality policy both in the international context and at the national level. This idea is enshrined in the Beijing Declaration and Platform for Action of the Fourth World Conference on Women. Further, Chapter 4, "Objectives and actions," states, "devise suitable statistical means to recognize and make visible the full extent of the work of women and all their contributions to the national economy, including their contribution in the unremunerated and domestic sectors, and examine the relationship of women's unremunerated work to the incidence of and their vulnerability to poverty" (United Nations 1996, 25).

Many countries have strived to make the volume of unpaid work visible using time use survey data, and some have also attempted to calculate the economic value of unpaid work in monetary terms, so that it can be compared with the national gross domestic product (GDP).

The Japanese government started measuring the monetary value of unpaid work in 1996. Currently, unpaid work is measured using the input approach, where the time input in hours is valued by multiplying it with an appropriate wage rate. Three methods are used by the Japanese government to calculate the monetary value of unpaid work:

1. The opportunity cost (OC) method values an individual's unpaid working time at the wage rate they are entitled to expect at the labor market.

The Japanese government calculations use the average wage of female workers, which of course reflects gender inequality in the labor market and is lower than the average wage of men. If this method, were applied separately to men and women, the value of men's contribution would higher than that of women, reflecting the gender wage gap.

2. The market replacement cost (RC) method values unpaid services at the price at which these services can be purchased in the market (Swiebel 1999). A *general substitute* (RC-G) is the wage of someone who can perform all the household tasks. In this method, the monetary value of unpaid work is estimated using the average wage of domestic workers.
3. Another method of measuring the market RC uses *specialized substitutes* (RC-S): it assumes that individuals with different occupational qualifications or training perform different household tasks (i.e., as cooks, cleaners, or nurses, etc). Regarding the calculation of the monetary value of caring work for the elderly, the average wage of paid home care workers is used to value unpaid care work.

Figure 1 depicts the results of the measurement of unpaid work in 2001 and 2006, as reported by the Japanese Cabinet Office (2013).

In general, the OC method estimates a total higher value of unpaid work than both the RC-S and RC-G (OECD 1995). Eurostat (2003, 26) argued that the RC-generalist approach is more appropriate since the working conditions of domestic workers and the contents of their work are similar to

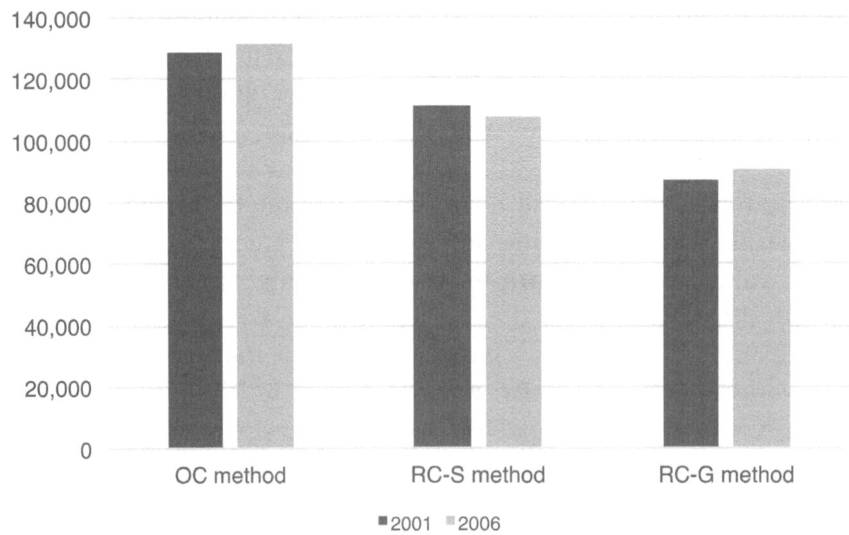

Figure 1. Monetary valuation of unpaid work in Japan during 2001 and 2006 (in billion yen) (Cabinet office 2003). RC-G method, replacement cost-generalist method; RC-S method, replacement cost-specialist method; OC method, opportunity cost method.

those of housework. This method gives the lowest total value, reflecting the low wages of domestic workers. The calculation using *specialized substitutes*, also reflects labor market inequalities as these workers' have lower wages than the average. Thus the difference between the results produced by the three methods is accounted for by labor market inequalities.[1] The OC method seems to be superior to the RC method in that the former estimates the valuation of unpaid work based on the average wages of female workers.[2] None of these market-based valuations captures fully the real value of unpaid work, taking account of the importance of the contribution it makes to the economy and to society.

The volume and value of care and domestic work

Regarding the valuation of paid care and domestic work, the System of National Accounts considers the wage paid in the market reflects the productive contribution of this work. However, feminist scholars have argued wages do not depend on productivity: low wages are paid to women because of the unequal bargaining position of women (Beechey 1987) and the wage paid for care and domestic work is low because women often do similar work without payment as wives and mothers. Moreover, if the government does not subsidize their employment, the wages of domestic workers employed by households will have to be less than what their female employer earns in the labor market (ILO 2010, 7).

The ILO (2011b) report titled "Measuring the economic and social value of domestic work" suggests that the value of paid domestic work to the workers themselves can be estimated comparing the "mean (or median) earnings of domestic workers with earnings of all other earners, including employers, the self-employed and employees" or "Alternatively, one could compare mean (or median) earnings of domestic workers with those of all other employees." The report clarifies that this method reveals "what a domestic worker might earn if she was doing another job" (ILO 2011b, 4–5). Another approach is to measure the value of the domestic worker to the household that employs them in terms of the economic value of the time freed up: "The suggested approach for this involves estimating the earnings received by a woman when she employs a domestic worker to do the domestic work so that the employing woman can engage in paid work elsewhere." (ILO 2011b, 6).

Both the methods proposed by the ILO enable us to recognize the gap between the actual wages received by domestic workers and the average wages of female or male workers in any other industry. This gap can be considered the penalty incurred by domestic workers in undertaking domestic work rather than some other work. In the global context, the receiving countries owe migrant workers recompense for the penalty reflected by the gap, since many workers in the host countries are only available in the labor market due to the essential services offered by domestic workers.

Gender equality policy and unpaid care and domestic work

Swiebel (1999, 17–19) considered four specific policies regarding unpaid work to be part of gender equality policy:

1. Promoting equal sharing of unpaid work between women and men
2. Introducing changes in the organization of paid employment to facilitate the individual combination of paid and unpaid work by both women and men
3. The provision of public services, such as childcare facilities
4. The commercialization of domestic labor, which governments can support by tax deductions or transfers (subsidies) to trades such as laundries, cleaning services, and repair and maintenance services.

In her argument, both the provision of public services and commercialization of domestic services are considered gender equality policies. However, the different effects of these two policies on people who do care and domestic work for pay have been rarely considered in discussions on gender equality.

Research on the welfare state has focused on the public provision of care as a measure to realize a gender-equal society. In a study on the welfare regime, Esping-Andersen (1999) used the term "de-familializing" regime defined as increasing public provision of childcare and elderly care. The proportion of the welfare budget allocated for social expenditure and the coverage of the services mentioned above is considered a significant de-familializing indicator. More specific concepts such as "care regime" (Daly 2001) focus on the distribution of care work among the state, market, community, and family. For instance, Daly (2001) analyzed European countries' care regimes using the data on the coverage of public care services for both children and the elderly and the cash benefits for family care during parental leave or caring for the elderly. Nordic countries such as Norway, Sweden, and Denmark are classified as "caring states," where the government provides both services and cash benefits, whereas Germany, France, Austria, and Belgium are classified as "pro-family caring states," where the government's care service coverage is low and families provide most of the care.

The focus on the state provision for care services as an indicator of gender equality becomes significant when it is a publicly financed infrastructure with public sector employment. However, domestic work that offers care and domestic services has not increased in the private sector supported by cash-payment policies. Italy, which is considered a "familistic Mediterranean country," has benefit schemes such as care allowances for dependent persons, and has deployed the marketized forms of care over recent decades (Bettio, Simonazzi, and Villa 2006, 272). Furthermore, low-paid marketized care provided by migrant workers has increased even in countries where such services are provided by the state, as state provision is insufficient (Shutes and Chiatti 2012): United Kingdom, Finland, and France have introduced cash payments or tax credits to assist citizens in employing child care workers in the home, and Sweden has introduced tax breaks for costs attributed to the employment of domestic workers (Williams 2012). These policies may lead to an "informal care-led model" (Pavolini and Ranci 2008), although in Sweden many domestic workers have formal contracts. Cash benefits like tax credits or tax breaks for the cost incurred in outsourcing unpaid care and domestic work are introduced since such a scheme effectively reduces the burden of unpaid work using a smaller budget than a scheme in which the state provides the service. This is further encouraged by a migration policy that increases the supply of workers who work for low wages.

The marketization of care and domestic work and gender equality in Sweden and Asian countries

The case of Sweden

Sweden has been praised as a "women-friendly state" that successfully implemented a long-term gender equal policy by employing care workers as public employees. Childcare and elderly care workers, as well as cleaners, were hired as public employees in the 1980s. However, over the years, privatization and outsourcing of the public sector's responsibilities have changed the welfare state to a more market-oriented one; tax breaks have been introduced for employers of domestic workers and these market mechanisms have widened the income gap among women.

As early as 1993, Ann-Marie Pålsson of the Conservative Party proposed tax deduction for expenses of employing domestic workers to promote gender equality in the labor market and reduce unpaid work in the household. The proponents argued the scheme would reduce the need for public services, encourage the individuals to purchase the services of domestic workers, and decrease informal work while increasing formal and legitimate work. Social Democrats criticized this scheme as one that would increase the number of low wage workers and widen class inequality.

In 2007, following the heated "maid debate," Sweden introduced a tax credit of 50% for the cost of hiring services of domestic workers. This tax credit is mainly used to purchase cleaning services from formal cleaning businesses (Bowman and Alyson 2014). At the time, the cleaning industry comprised many small firms; however, from 2007 onward, several large cleaning firms started business (Bowman and Alyson 2014). After the enactment of the scheme, it is reported that cleaning remains a feminized and ethnically segregated low-income and low-status occupation; the employment is often part-time, not because workers have chosen this, but because of the schedules demanded by the clients (Abbasian and Hellgren 2012, 165). Alongside the formal market for domestic services, Sweden continues to accommodate informal, undocumented, self-employed migrant domestic workers (Hobson, Hellgren, and Bede 2015, 49).

Since high-income, elderly persons are overrepresented as buyers of cleaning services, the tax credit scheme constitutes an upward redistribution of resources to households with more resources already (Hobson, Hellgren, and Bede 2015). This unequalizing effect was also observed between households with children; those who used the tax discount were characterized by substantially higher individual labor earnings and higher family disposable incomes compared to those who did not use the discount (Halldén and Stenberg 2018). Analysis based on the Swedish population register data for 2000–2010 shows that outsourcing of domestic work (mainly housework, not child care) by married women, corresponding on average to 2.0–3.5% of full-time work (40–70 h per year), increased the labor market work of married women, leading to an average increase of 2.4–3.6% in their annual earnings (Halldén and Stenberg 2018). Further, it reveals that the tax deduction for the outsourcing of domestic work reduced the earnings gender gap for highly skilled women but had little effect on the gender gap for the earnings of women from lower social classes.

The case of Sweden proves that using a tax credit to reduce the cost of the purchase of domestic services promoted gender equality for white, heterosexual, working mothers (Kvist and Peterson 2010), while it widened the income gap between women who can and cannot afford to buy these services.[3] These gaps could affect gender equality in the following way. The individuals that cannot afford to purchase the marketized service, even when covered by a tax deduction, will have to shoulder the unpaid work by cutting down on their worker's sleep or reducing their working hours in the labor market. Even today, female workers in the middle- or lower-income households face "time poverty" in juggling unpaid and paid work

(Fraser 2016), whereas rich female workers are relatively free from time poverty. The gender equality promoted by marketization widens the income gap among women based on ethnic and class differences.

The case of Asian countries

In discussions on welfare regimes, Asian countries are called familialistic states since they do not have much welfare provision, which means the family's role is crucial in providing care and doing domestic work (Ochiai 2019). Asian countries like Singapore, Hong Kong, and Taiwan facilitated migrant workers to undertake care and domestic work to support an increase in labor market participation of their female citizens. The increase in the participation rate of local female workers resulting from employing migrant workers in their homes is estimated to be 10.6% in Hong Kong, 13.9% in Singapore, and 2.6% in Taiwan (Asato 2015, 275). To some extent, Singapore is reported to have a gender-equal society and ranks 20th in Economic Participation and Opportunity in the Gender Gap Index 2020 (World Economic Forum 2020). However, at the same time, there are 210,000 migrant domestic workers in the country, which has approximately 5.64 million residents. Since the introduction of the Foreign Maid Scheme in 1987, migrant domestic workers have been mainly female workers from Indonesia or the Philippines (Asato 2015). In Taiwan, the numbers of migrant domestic workers grew from approximately 700 in 1992 to 255,000 in 2019, and the Taiwanese female labor force participation rate increased from 44.83% in 1992 to 51.27% in 2019, sustained by the labor provided by domestic workers (Ogawa 2019, 246). In so far as the utilization of marketized domestic work increases female labor force participation, it is likely to contribute to national economic growth and gender equality in the labor market. In addition, there is a clearer conflict of interest between the user of the services and the domestic worker since the users directly employ domestic workers in these countries.[4] We can illustrate the effect of direct employment by households on domestic workers' working conditions by considering the case of Singapore.

First, it is rational for households, as employers, to control their expenses by keeping down worker's wages. Moreover, the wages of domestic workers in Singapore are low compared to the wages in Hong Kong and Taiwan, mainly due to the nation's "Foreign Worker Levy (FWL)" on the employment of migrant workers (JILPT 2015). Households that employ migrant domestic workers are expected to pay between 265 Singapore dollars per month to the government. In general, the conflict of interest between the employer and workers are mitigated by the benefit from the government. The Singapore government recently reduced the amount of FWL for households with children below 12 years or elderly above 65 years of age, and more households have started employing domestic workers.

Second, since the regulations established for limiting working hours and the provision of minimum wages for domestic workers are weak, a household that directly employs domestic workers benefit from the ability to enforce long hours of work and paying less than the minimum wage. In Singapore, employers can expect live-in domestic workers, who are separated from their community and home, to perform 24 h of flexible work since migrant domestic workers are exempted from the labor law and regulations regarding the provision of time off and minimum wages.

This section explored how the marketization of care and domestic work and utilization of female migrant workers has been supported by both "caring states" like Sweden and by "familialistic states" in Asian countries. There is a conflict of interest between domestic workers and the households to which they supply services, especially if the households are the employers of the domestic workers. This conflict may be eased if the government covers the cost of the services and pays the wages for workers who supply care and domestic services to households. However, the Japanese case in the next section illustrates that care and domestic workers are underpaid even in publicly funded services.

The marketization of work in the publicly funded care system in Japan

The marketization of care services

Japan has been categorized as a familialistic state since its care service coverage is low but it has been supporting an increase in provision of care services to elderly people in their own homes, as they become too frail to take care of themselves and do their own housework.

In the 1960s and 1970s, care workers were considered public employees and were paid wages directly by local governments at rates determined by local governments. However, in the 1980s, local governments started outsourcing care work to voluntary associations and private companies, and wages were paid as outsourcing costs (Yamane 2020). In 1997, the government adopted a price by case contract based on the unit of service cost. A study comparing the costs of local government services to private care services revealed that the commission costs for private agencies were 30–60% of the commission costs for local government services (Chihou Jichi Keieigakkai 1997). For this reason, the service was privatized and outsourced to increase the number of services and control expenditure increases. Furthermore, the government role changed from a provider to a supervisor who controlled the market-supplied quantity and quality of care in the care facilities and home care services.

The introduction of Long Term Care Insurance (LTCI) in 2000 significantly changed the Japanese elderly care sector. It is widely believed that the LTCI established citizens' right to use the universal service, as it ensures that the financial resources of the service are sustained by a premium on taxes paid by citizens. With the LTCI system, citizens above 40 years old pay the premium for long-term care as part of their health insurance while citizens above 65 pay it through a deduction from their pension. They are entitled to use the services by paying 10 or 20% of the service cost depending on their income level and can use the kind of service depending on their health condition.[5]

The LTCI was strongly supported by feminist thinkers who expected it to increase care services and reduce women's unpaid care work provided for elderly kin. However, feminists who appreciated the system's merit from the position of users have not yet thoroughly discussed the devaluation of wages of care workers under the LTCI. Under the marketized policy, the hourly wage for home care workers has decreased over the past 30 years, even as service provision has increased. For example, a report by the Cabinet Office (2013) specified that an hourly wage of 1759 yen for home care workers under RC-specialist substitutes was used for valuing unpaid work in 1996, while the hourly wage used for this calculation declined to 1193 yen in 2011.[6] The marketization of these services has degraded the value of care workers' wages during this period.

The provision of low wages for care workers in the LTCI system

The LTCI system has created a quasi-market where nonprofit and profit undertakings participate on an equal footing; this market is supposed to encourage a more efficient distribution of resources by facilitating competition among providers through the choices by the users, unlike the public service. However, there is no competition for the service price among providers in this quasi-market because the LTCI fee is set as an official price by the government according to the type of the care provided. The providers have to cover their costs and profits with fixed fee that the local government pays to them: they decide what the workers pay should be. The LTCI fee for care services has been continuously reduced over the last 20 years and the fee does not take into account what the cost of monthly wages for home care workers would be if it were based on average hourly wages for regular workers. Therefore, the providers hire most workers as non-regular workers who are only paid hourly wages. Moreover, in the LTCI system, services to homes are divided into "physical care" and low-priced "housework." Physical care includes bathing and assisting in the toilet needs of the elderly, while low-priced housework includes household

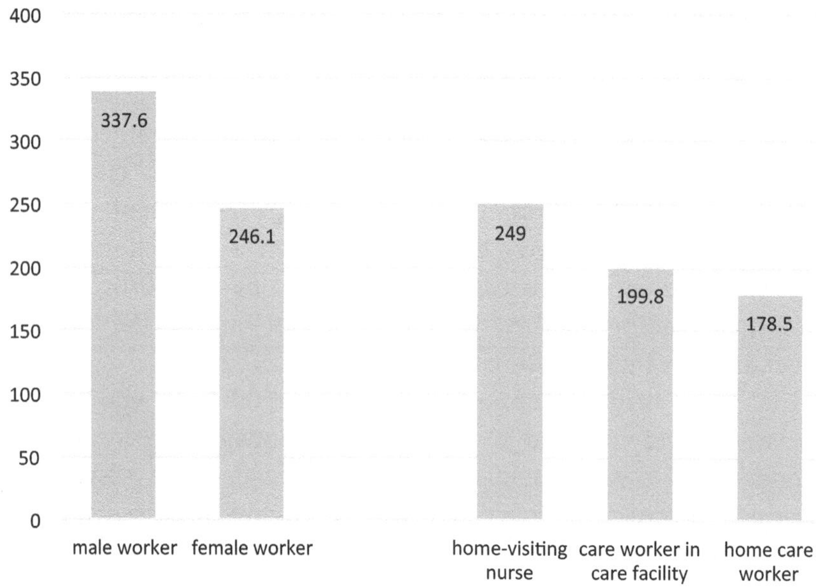

Figure 2. Monthly averages of male and female workers in all industries and of care workers in 2018 (in thousand yen) (CWF 2018; MHLW 2018a).

chores like washing, cooking, cleaning the house, etc. Though most home care worker provides both physical care and housework, the low-priced housework service lowers the wages of home care workers. Though most home care worker provides both physical care and housework, the low-priced housework service lowers the wages of home care workers. Figure 2 depicts the wage gaps between care workers of different types and full time workers averaged across all industries (MHLW 2018a; CWF 2018).

These data reveal that home care workers' wages are lower than those of workers in care facilities workers and home-visiting nurses. The LTCI law of 2018 stipulated the housework service per 45 min to be 181 units (since 1 unit is equivalent to 10 yen, the fee of housework service per 45 min is approximately 1,810 yen), physical care per 30 min to be 248 units, and home-visiting nursing per 30 min to be 467 units. The valuation of home-visiting nursing services, undertaken by nurses with national nursing qualifications, is 3.9 times that of housework services. Since the provider must cover the cost of clerical work and other managerial costs from the total amount of the LTCI fees received before the care workers are paid, the average hourly wage amount for home care workers who provides both physical care and housework is only 1,162 yen (CWF 2018).

In the qualification system of care workers, home care work, which includes housework, is categorized as the least skilled work. Individuals can qualify as home care workers even with low-level professional qualifications, which require them only to take a course. In contrast, care facility workers must achieve a higher level of professional qualification, which requires them to pass a national examination. It is evident that home care work under the LTCI system has been completely feminized; a low monetary value is placed on it because women undertake such work without payment, and its status as non-regular work is legitimized by the fact that women have or had undertaken unpaid work in their households. Gutiérrez-Rodríguez (2010) argued that feminization of labor has a twofold meaning: (1) the devaluation of work in sectors where women are overrepresented and (2) the incorporation of skills and capabilities that are traditionally associated with women as carers. The concept of feminization of labor suggests that domestic work is devalued and deskilled because it is offered by female workers.

Since 80% of the home care workers are non-regular workers who work for an hourly wage of 1,162 yen (CWF 2018), their average monthly income is 108,000 yen, roughly one-third of the average wage of full-time male workers. Statistics data show that the average working hours for non-regular workers per week are 23 h. Moreover, this obscures the considerable number of unpaid hours that are worked by non-regular home care workers. The wage is paid for only the actual time spent providing the service in the user's house, and it does not account for the traveling time and waiting time spent by the workers. Studies on home care workers have revealed that "incidental working hours," which include workers' traveling time, waiting time, and time for reporting, meeting, and training, comprise 36% of the time spent by non-regular workers in their work (Tsuboi 2015).

The unpaid incidental working hours have increased due to the government's continuous efforts to reform the LTCI to shorten the duration of home care service visits. For instance, the duration of housework service visits was shortened from 1.5 h in 2003 to 1 h in 2006 and 45 min in 2012, whilst the duration of physical care services have also been reduced but not by as much.[7] The homecare work in Japan became similar to "time and task" care in the UK, which also pursues cost-effectiveness in a quasi-market (Lewis and Glennerster 1996)

The shortening of the duration of visits increased workers' travel time spent on proceeding to the next home since home care workers had to visit more users within a single day than before the implementation of the LTCI reform. In addition, workers perform unpaid overtime work to listen to users' needs and satisfy their expectations for conversation (Yamane 2014). Unions report that 40% of the workers believe that their "incomes have decreased" due to the shortening of the time allowed for each visit (NCTU 2013).

The reform has been implemented on the pretext of controlling social welfare expenditure in an aging society. However, it has fundamental problems. The monthly wage of a home care worker is not calculated in the

LTCI fee, and the providers cannot cover wages for incidental working hours with the LTCI fee. Finally, home care workers filed a state compensation suit because LTCI fees do not guarantee that they are paid the minimum wage which each local authority stipulates. The plaintiff reported that although it took 9 h and 35 min (575 min) from her arrival to her departure from the office each day, the time considered in her wages is only 285 min. Even when the 60-min lunchtime is subtracted from the remainder of 290 min; her work for 230 min remains unpaid and amounts to 40% of her total working hours (Nishimura 2019). This case revealed the extent to which home care workers are underpaid.[8]

The public or private agencies did not gain much from these low wages because the LTCI fee was too low to permit much profit. These fees are paid from taxation (the LTCI premium) and the tax should be sufficient to cover home care workers' expenses, and provide them with at least the minimum wage, even if it is outsourced work.

Discussion and conclusion: how we value unpaid and paid care and domestic and work

This study discusses how the gender inequality implications of paid care and domestic work have been overlooked in the discussion of gender equality policies. The situations of underpaid care workers and domestic workers are at the core of the intersection of gender and class inequality. The growth of underpaid care and domestic work has been created by marketization policies to increase services to replace unpaid care and domestic work introduced both by "caring states" and by "familialistic states." In the countries considered in this paper, the expansion of marketized care and domestic work supports national economic growth and improvements in average levels of gender equality in the labor market while minimizing additional costs to the state (Ehrenreich and Hochschild 2003). Just as unpaid work subsidizes public-sector provisioning (Antonopoulos 2009), paid care and domestic work also subsidizes public sector provisioning, through being underpaid. However, in all cases, the full contribution of care and domestic work to the economy at the national level remains partly unrecognized. Finding an appropriate approach for valuing unpaid and underpaid care work and domestic work to bridge income gaps not only between women and men but among women are fundamental for feminist discussions. Based on the above discussion, I propose the following three feminist initiatives.

First, if the feminist valuation of unpaid work aims to make the contributions and burdens of women visible, we must know the contributions and burdens of the paid but undervalued care and domestic workers. Accordingly, I put forward the following propositions:

1. We can combine time use surveys for unpaid care and domestic work and paid care and domestic work and make visible the total time spent in providing these services, including time spent in traveling to provide these services.
2. We can value care and domestic work by multiplying the amount of time care workers and domestic workers spend on these work by the average wage of workers in the country where the work is done.
3. It is important to recognize existing wage gaps between workers' average wages across industries and wages of care and domestic workers as indicators of gender inequality.

Second, we should find a way to ease the burden of unpaid work for women in any household regardless of family income levels. If the amount of the service which each household can use is decided by its purchasing power, this only widens the gap among women because affluent women can avail more of care services than poor ones. To reduce the gap between women who can afford to purchase care and domestic services and those who cannot, the costs to the users of services should be low and graduated according to household incomes, with the worse off households getting free services; the rest of the costs of providing services should be covered by general taxation. However, Hence, this is not a cash-payment system but an in-kind provision of care and domestic services like the public education system or public childcare system. This policy would make it easier for poor single parents to use care and domestic services than a system of deductions from income tax (like Sweden), and would ease the time poverty of non-wealthy women and encourage them to work in the labor market. Moreover, this encourages care and domestic services to be regarded not as commercial goods but as public goods that support gender and class equality in our society. With this logic, we can legitimize a system supported by all citizens through tax payments in their lifetime.

Third, we advocate raising the social and economic value of care and domestic work and close the income gap between these workers and those in other industries. One strategy to better value care and domestic work is to professionalize it.[9] Professionalization of this work through a qualification system would help to empower care and domestic workers. Since they cannot easily be evaluated by their productivity, their work is often to be evaluated by the subjective satisfaction of the users. This enables the users to make demands that are often excessive regarding the quality of services in the private sphere of their own home. Professionalization through a qualification system might increase the bargaining power of care and domestic workers and protect them from excessive demands by users of their services. Government controls the quality of care through a qualification system, with public inspections of providers, which could supersede market principles (e.g., competition, where the users choose the kind of providers they want) in securing the quality of services. To secure better pay and conditions for care and domestic workers in households, we need equality between the user and the worker to mutually respect the dignity and rights of the other. This should replace the model of a consumer-producer relationship under the marketized form of service provision.[9]

Another strategy in tandem with professionalization is to secure a living wage and better working conditions for care and domestic workers. The formalization and implementation of labor laws regulating the minimum wage, working hours, benefits in case of ill-health and leave for live-in workers are crucial. Moreover, as this study explains, while care and domestic workers may be formally protected by labor laws, their working conditions remain precarious, because they daily visit different clients and perform fragmented services. The government should develop a fixed wage for domestic workers as non-regular workers. Reports show that domestic workers who are directly employed by different clients and provide fragmented services have difficulty getting compensation when their health is compromised (Ohashi 2020, 127). This situation would be improved if workers can join providers or associations offering a fixed rate for their services, which would enable domestic workers to receive a stable income and benefits.

In addition, trade unions for care and domestic workers should be supported, allowing their advocacy at global and local levels (Anderson 2010; Lim 2016; Ito 2020), to aid the improvement of their working conditions and wages. Regarding the type of providers, for-profit companies distribute dividends to their shareholders, and are motivated to lower the labor costs and prioritize profits over workers' benefits. This is different in nonprofit organizations or associations. The ILO expects to enhance the role of cooperatives among care and domestic workers to increase wages and offer stable employment. The cooperatives play an intermediary role so that workers can find an alternative to joining private employment agencies (ILO 2013, 5).[10]

Feminists should call for a system of service provision that raises the valuation of care and domestic work, paid and unpaid, and seek collaboration with relevant associations to help raise the wages of such workers.

Disclosure statement

No potential conflict of interest was reported by the author(s).

Notes

1. We face the same problem even if we use the output approach. In this approach, the value of unpaid work is calculated based on the outcomes of unpaid production by assigning a price to the quantities of goods and services produced in the market. The value of the output of care work is calculated by multiplying the time used for caring for one child or elderly person by the wage of the substitute carer (Hashimoto 2014, 126).
2. According to some researchers, the OC method is not appropriate because it uses the average wage of a female or male worker for calculation, whereas the problem can be solved using the average wage for workers, both male and female, across industries. The Japanese government calculated the unpaid work of women by female worker's average wages, and that of men by male worker's average wages.
3. Research conducted in the United States also revealed that low-skilled immigration increases the average hours of market work per week for working women in the top quartile of female wage distribution; however, it has no effect on the average market work hours for women with wages below the median value (Cortés and Tessada 2011, 2).
4. In Taiwan, the government applied labor laws to migrant workers; however, this step was withdrawn due to employers' opposition to the proposed increase in wages of domestic workers (Asato 2015, 279).
5. The premium of citizens above 40 under 65 not participating in the labor market is covered by the health insurance associations to which their household head belongs.
6. The former is the wage of a full-time home care worker, which was directly subsidized by the state, and the latter is the average wage of home care workers and home-visiting nurses.
7. The minimum duration of physical care has decreased from 30 min in 2003 to 20 min in 2012. Physical care is commonly offered along with housework services, before or after the housework service.
8. The case is pending in court as of 2021.
9. For example, a workers' cooperative in New York realized the value of a training program for migrant nannies where they get to improve their communication skills in English (Mori 2020). By this they can change the power relation with the users by formal recognition of their skill and profession.
10. ILO defines cooperative as "an autonomous association of persons united voluntarily to meet common economic, social and cultural needs through a democratically controlled enterprise" (ILO 2010, 3).

Funding

This work was supported by the JSPS KAKENHI under Grant Number JP 20K02071.

References

Abbasian, Saeid, and Carina Hellgren. 2012. "Working Conditions for Female and Immigrant Cleaners in Stockholm County—an Intersectional Approach." *Nordic Journal of Working Life Studies* 2 (3):161–181. doi:10.19154/njwls.v2i3.2369.

Anderson, Bridget. 2010. "Mobilizing Migrants, Making Citizens: Migrant Domestic Workers as Political Agents." *Ethnic and Racial Studies* 33 (1):60–74. doi:10.1080/01419870903023660.

Antonopoulos, Rania. 2009. *The Unpaid Care Work—Paid Work Connection*. Working paper no. 86. Geneva: International Labour Office, Policy Integration and Statistics Department.

Asato, Wako. 2015. "Imin Regimu ga Teikisuru Mondai" [the Issue That Migrant Regime Bring Up]." *The Quarterly of Social Security Research* 15 (3–4):270–286. http://www.ipss.go.jp/syoushika/bunken/data/pdf/20143603.pdf

Barrett, Michelle. 1980. *Women's Oppression Today. Problems in Marxist Feminist Analysis*. London: Verso.

Beechey, Veronica. 1987. *Unequal Work*. London: Verso.

Bettio, Francesca, Annamaria Simonazzi, and Paola Villa. 2006. "Change in Care Regimes and Female Migration: The Care Drain in the Mediterranean." *Journal of European Social Policy* 16 (3):271–285. doi:10.1177/0958928706065598.

Bowman, John R., and M. Cole Alyson. 2014. "Cleaning the 'People's Home': The Politics of the Domestic Service Market in Sweden." *Gender, Work & Organization* 21 (2): 187–201. doi:10.1111/gwao.12029.

Cabinet Office 2013. Kajikatshdoutou no hyouka nituite 2011nendeta niyoru saisuikei [Evaluation of Housework etc. Re-estimation by Data on 2011]. https://www.esri.cao.go.jp/jp/sna/sonota/satellite/roudou/contents/kajikatsudoutou.html

Chihou Jichi Keieigakkai, 1997. "Koureisya fukushi no kanminkosuto wo hikaku" [a Comparison of the Cost of Public and Private Service]. *Jyunkan the Welfare of Employee* 1592:21–23.

Cortés, Patricia, and Jose Tessada. 2011. "Low-Skilled Immigration and the Labor Supply of Highly Skilled Women." *American Economic Journal: Applied Economics* 3 (3):88–123. doi:10.1257/app.3.3.88.

CWF (Care Work Foundation). 2018. "Kaigo Roudou Jittai Chosa" [Survey on Care Workers]. http://www.kaigo-center.or.jp/report/2019_chousa_01.html

Dalla Costa, Mariarosa, and Selma James. 1972. *The Power of Women and the Subversion of the Community*. London: Butler and Tanner.

Daly, Mary. 2001. "Care Policies in Western Europe." In *Care Work: The Quest for Security*, edited by Mary Daly, 33–35. Geneva: International Labour Office.

Ehrenreich, Barbara, and Arlie R. Hochschild. 2003. *Global Women: Nannies, Maids, and Sex Workers in the New Economy*. New York: Metropolitan.

Elson, Diane. 2017. "Recognize, Reduce, Redistribute Unpaid Care Work: How to Close the Gender Gap." *New Labor Forum* 26 (2):52–61. doi:10.1177/1095796017700135.

Esping-Andersen, Gosta. 1999. *Social Foundations of Postindustrial Economies*. Oxford: Oxford University Press.

Eurostat 2003. *Household Production and consumption - Proposal for a Methodology of the Household Satellite Accounts*. Luxembourg: Office for Official Publication of the European Communities.

Fraser, Nancy. 2016. "Contradictions of Capital and Care." *New Left Review* 100:99–117. https://newleftreview.org/issues/II100/articles/nancy-fraser-contradictions-of-capital-and-care.

Gutiérrez-Rodríguez, E. 2010. *Migration, Domestic Work and Affect*. London: Routledge.

Halldén, Karin, and Anders Stenberg. 2018. "The Relationship Between Hours of Outsourced Domestic Services and Female Earnings: Evidence from a Swedish Tax

Reform." *Research in Social Stratification and Mobility* 55:120–133. doi:10.1016/j.rssm.2018.04.003.

Hashimoto, Miyuki. 2014. *Musyouroudouhyouka no houhou oyobi seisaku tono thunagari* [Approach to Valuation of Unpaid Work and the Relation with Policy]. Tokyo: Sangyoutoukeikennkyuusya.

Hobson, Barbara, Zenia Hellgren, and Luwam Bede. 2015. "How Institutional Contexts Matter: Migration and Domestic Services and the Capabilities of Migrants in Spain and Sweden." Families and Societies Working Paper Series 46. http://www.familiesandsocieties.eu/wp-content/uploads/2015/11/WP46HobsonEtAl2015.pdf

ILO. 2010. *Report IV (1): Decent Work for Domestic Workers.* International Labour Conference, 99th Session, 2010. Geneva: International Labour Office. https://www.ilo.org/ilc/ILCSessions/previous-sessions/99thSession/reports/WCMS_104700/lang–en/index.htm

ILO. 2011a. *Decent Work for Domestic Workers from International Labor Conference Previous Sessions.* Geneva: International Labour Office. https://www.ilo.org/ilc/ILCSessions/previous-sessions/100thSession/on-the-agenda/decent-work-for-domestic-workers/lang–en/index.htm

ILO. 2011b. *Domestic Work Policy Brief No. 3: Measuring the Economic and Social Value of Domestic Work.* Geneva: International Labour Office. https://www.ilo.org/travail/whatwedo/publications/WCMS_156071/lang–en/index.htm

ILO. 2013. *Global Mapping of Domestic Worker Cooperatives and Social and Solidarity Economy Organizations.* Geneva: International Labour Office. http://www.ilo.org/dyn/migpractice/docs/198/global

Ito, Ruri. 2020. *Kaji Roudou no Kokusai Shakaigaku* [Transnational Sociology of Domestic Work: In Quest of Decent Work]. Kyoto: Jinbunsyoin.

JILPT (Japan Institute for Labour Policy and Training). 2015. "Trends in Accepting Foreign Workers in Major Countries: Singapore." January 2015. https://www.jil.go.jp/foreign/labor_system/2015_01/singapore.html

Kvist, Elin, and Elin Peterson. 2010. "What Has Gender Equality Got to Do with It? An Analysis of Policy Debates Surrounding Domestic Services in the Welfare States of Spain and Sweden." *Nora - Nordic Journal of Feminist and Gender Research* 18 (3):185–203. doi:10.1080/08038740.2010.498326.

Lewis, Jane, and Howard Glennerster. 1996. *Implementing the New Community Care.* Buckingham: Open University Press.

Lim, Adelyn. 2016. "Transnational Organising and Feminist Politics of Difference and Solidarity: The Mobilisation of Domestic Workers in Hong Kong." *Asian Studies Review* 40 (1):70–88. doi:10.1080/10357823.2015.1124841.

MHLW (Ministry of Health, Labor and Welfare). 2018a. *Chingin kouzou kihon toukei chosa* [Basic Survey on Wage Structure]. https://www.mhlw.go.jp/english/database/db-l/ordinary.html

MHLW (Ministry of Health, Labor and Welfare) 2018b. *Hiseikikoyou no genjyo to Kadai* [Condition and Problem of Non-Regular Employment]. https://www.mhlw.go.jp/content/000501869.pdf

Mori, Chikako. 2020. "Ijyuujyosei no enpawamento to chiiki komyunitysoshiki no akuwari" [Empowerment of Migrant Women and the Role of Organization of Local Community]." In *Kaji Roudou no Kokusai Shakaigaku* [Transnational Sociology of Domestic Work: In Quest of Decent Work], edited by Ruri Ito, 289–314. Kyoto: Jinbunsyoin.

NCTU (National Confederation of Trade Unions) 2013. "Zenrouren herupa anketo" [The Survey on the Home Care Workers]. http://www.cwac.jp/blog/files/2013helper_anq.pdf

Nishimura, Hitomi. 2019. "Tachiagaru homu herupa tachi" [the Home Helpers Who Are Taking Action." *Shukan Kinyoubi* 1248:46–48.

Ochiai, Emiko. 2019. "Ajia' to 'Nihon' no saiteigi" [Redefining "Asia" and "Japan" Creating an Intellectual Foundation for Academic Collaboration within Asia." *Japan Sociological Review* 70 (3):200–221.

OECD. 1995. *Household Production in OECD Countries: Data Source and Measurement Methods*. Paris: OECD. http://www.oecd.org/sdd/na/2674378.pdf

Ogawa, Reiko. 2019. "Higashi Ajia niokeru Ijyuukearoudousya no Kouchiku" [Constructing Migrant Care Workers in East Asia."] *Japan Sociological Review* 70 (3):241–263.

Ohashi, Fumie. 2020. "Honkon syakai no kaji roudousya" [Domesic Workers in Hong Kong]. In *Kaji Roudou no Kokusai Shakaigaku* [Transnational Sociology of Domestic Work: In Quest of Decent Work], edited by Ruri Ito, 289–314. Kyoto: Jinbunsyoin.

Pavolini, Emmanuele, and Costanzo Ranci. 2008. "Restructuring the Welfare State: Reforms in Long-Term Care in Western European Countries." *Journal of European Social Policy* 18 (3):246–259. doi:10.1177/0958928708091058.

Shutes, Isabel, and Carlos Chiatti. 2012. "Migrant Labour and the Marketisation of Care for Older People: The Employment of Migrant Care Workers by Families and Service Providers." *Journal of European Social Policy* 22 (4):392–405. doi:10.1177/0958928712449773.

Swiebel, Joke. 1999. "Unpaid Work and Policy-Making Towards a Broader Perspective of Work and Employment." ST/ESA/1999/DP.4DESA Discussion Paper 4. https://www.un.org/esa/desa/papers/1999/esa99dp4.pdf

Tsuboi, Yosifumi. 2015. "Houmonkaigo niokeru futairoudoujikan nithuiteno kenkyu" [The Study on "Incidental Working Hours in the Home Help Service" of Home Care Work]. Departmental Bulletin Paper of Kyoto Prefectural University 7:77–96. http://id.nii.ac.jp/1122/00000079/

United Nations 1996. "Beijing Declaration and Platform for Action." https://www.un.org/en/events/pastevents/pdfs/Beijing_Declaration_and_Platform_for_Action.pdf

Williams, Fiona. 2012. "Converging Variation in Migrant Care Work in Europe." *Journal of European Social Policy* 22 (4):363–376. doi:10.1177/0958928712449771.

World Economic Forum. 2020. *Global Gender Gap Report*. https://www.weforum.org/reports/global-gender-gap-report-2020

Yamane, Sumika. 2014. "Kaigohokenkaniokeru homuherupuroudou no henka" [the Changes of Home Care Work under the Long Term Care Insurance: The Task Based Work in the Practice of Individual Care." *Annual Report of the Japanese Association of Labor Sociology* 25:3–21.

Yamane, Sumika. 2020. "Formal Care Work under the Japanese Quasi-Market: Toward a Care Friendly Gender Regime." In *Handbook of East Asian Gender Studies*, edited by Jieyu Liu and Junko Yamashita, 169–184. London: Routledge.

Development, gender, and asymmetries between Mexico and Japan

Alicia Girón

ABSTRACT

The gender gaps in Mexico and Japan can be fruitfully compared even though the economic development of these two countries is at very different levels. The purpose of this paper is to compare gender equity between a developed and an underdeveloped country through a comparative and descriptive analysis using gender and macroeconomic indexes. The World Economic Forum points out that Mexico was ranked 75th and Japan 80th out of 153 countries on the Global Gender Gap Index in 2006, but by 2020 Mexico reached 25th place, and Japan had fallen to the 121st. In this paper, indicators and statistics will function as an aid in understanding gender gaps, macroeconomic differences, and the development of women in Mexico and Japan. The time reference for this study includes the periods before and after the Great International Financial Crisis (GFC), a watershed in global economic development until 2020.

Introduction

The 2030 Development Agenda, approved by the United Nations, placed gender equity as one of the Sustainable Development Goals (SDGs) while also looking to improve gender equity in the attainment of the other SDGs. The analysis and comparison of gender gaps between Mexico and Japan is illuminating in the global, regional, and national contexts because of the close relationship of gender gaps to the public policies in both countries.

Over the last few decades, one of the major contributions of feminist economics has been the incorporation of the gender dimension in the fields of macroeconomics and microeconomics as well as its impact in monitoring the economic development of women through the gender indicators developed by international organizations like the United Nations (UN), International Monetary Fund (IMF), World Bank (WB), International Labor Organization (ILO), and the World Economic Forum (WEF). It is important to highlight that there is a causal relationship between the outcomes measured by these indicators and the public policies created to reduce gender gaps.

Chizuko Ueno (1998) observed a decreasing trend in the birth rate in Japan together with an increased inclusion of women in the labor market under the industrialization policy of the 1950s and 1960s. The policy response included "… daycare facilities […] meant for working mothers, not for children. And actually, the first beneficiaries of this policy were the companies that hired women workers. It was these companies that should have taken responsibility for providing child care as a cost of employing women workers. They benefited from public services by not having to spend the money for child care on their premises" (Ueno 1998, 125).

The financial imbalances during the late 1980s and early 1990s, together with the unprecedented collapse of the real estate bubble, needed the central Bank of Japan (BoJ) to control the financial crisis and aim for price stability. However, despite the use of unconventional monetary policies deflation was not avoided. The "… monetary-fiscal policy coordination has been hampered by the absence of an effective commitment mechanism" (Westelius, 2020, 19). High public debt limited financial support, and the monetary stimulus was insufficient to exit deflation. Furthermore, the entire deflation[1] period laid the groundwork for such a weak growth process that a national care policy had to be formulated so that women faced fewer difficulties when joining the workforce.

In Japan, Prime Minister Shinzo Abe considered gender equality to be a key strategy to reactivate the economy along with monetary and fiscal policies; women's participation was seen as crucial to revitalizing the economy and drawing it out from its continuing low levels of growth. "Several decades of economic stagnation led Abe to spearhead a multi-faceted reform effort to shake off deflation and come to grips with Japan's large national debt and rapidly aging society" (Groysberg 2017). Investment in the care economy has been a central axis in favoring the incorporation of women into the labor force. "To support these efforts at effecting institutional change, Abe also has overseen rapid growth in daycare facilities for the children of working mothers and has worked intensively to encourage Japan's business associations to increase hiring, promoting, and empowering women among member enterprises" (Groysberg 2017). However, beyond the monetary policy to comply with the Abenomics program, whose third arrow points toward greater participation of women in public life, there was a lack of deep structural reforms looking to exit deflation and reduce gender gaps.

The participation of women in the workforce of Mexico increased substantially from the mid-seventies until 2020. The breakdown of the "stabilizing development" model, as a result of a major debt crisis, followed by the stabilization and austerity plans of the International Monetary Fund (IMF), caused economic difficulties that led to a growth in informal employment and a decrease in the wage rates of families' main providers. This created the need to expand the income of households and resulted in a drastic increase in the rate of women's participation in the labor market. This phenomenon was not exclusive to Mexico since it spread throughout Latin America, and in what is known as the "lost decade" of the 1980s.

The breakdown of the development model, which had yielded 8 percent growth rates in Mexico, led to an increase in migration from Mexico to the United States, which escalated after the signing of the Free Trade Agreement between Canada, United States, and Mexico (NAFTA). Even though there was a gradual change in the configuration of the traditional family (father, mother, and children) and the number of female providers and household heads in Mexico increased, there was a lack of investment in care services for women who worked either in the formal or informal sector. The Montevideo Strategy[2] Agreement identified four structural problems[3] that need to be addressed in Mexico and Latin America: (1) socioeconomic inequality and poverty; (2) cultural patriarchal discriminatory and/or violent patterns of behavior, and the culture of privilege[4]; (3) the sexual division of labor and an unfair social care organization, and (4) a concentration of power with hierarchical relationships within the public sphere.

This paper will first provide a brief review of the macroeconomic context and income inequality in Mexico and Japan; secondly, a comparison between the global gender gap indices and the underlying non-market gender asymmetries in Mexico and Japan; a comparison of gender inequalities related to wages in the labor markets and, lastly, financial and digital inclusion. The time period for this study includes the period before and after the Great Financial Crisis (GFC), up until 2020, a milestone of global economic development.

Macroeconomic context and income inequality

The GDP per capita is the primary macroeconomic indicator showing income inequality between countries with different development levels. According to the World Bank estimates (World Bank 2020), the GDP per capita per person in Japan was close to $48,919, while it was only $10,385 in Mexico during 2018. The GDP per capita gap between the two countries was close to $37,534. The level of GDP per capita in Japan was almost five times that of Mexico[5]. Both countries recorded a drop in GDP per capita 2009 following the GFC. Compared to 2008, there was a 5.4 percent drop in Japan, while there was a 6.6 percent drop in Mexico. However, Japan and Mexico registered an average increase of 16 percent and 12.2 percent GDP per capita, respectively, in the period 2000–2018.

Japan ranked as the fifth country in the Asia-Pacific Economic Cooperation (APEC) Forum with the highest per capita income only after Singapore ($58,247), Australia ($56,919), the United States ($54,541) and Canada ($51,357), while Mexico ranked 13th out of the 21 APEC countries[6] below the $24,328 average value, for which Mexico's per capita product was only 42.6 percent of the average member in 2018.

The fiscal and financial policies in Mexico and Japan may explain their difference and their inter-household income inequality can be measured using the Gini coefficient[7], whose behavior shows the same behavior for both in different periods. For the year 2000, the Gini coefficient was 0.50 for Mexico and 0.33 for Japan; in 2006, in Mexico it was 0.48, and Japan was 0.32; in 2012, in Mexico it was 0.46 and Japan 0.33; and, finally in 2018, Mexico's Gini coefficient was 0.46 and Japan's 0.23. Thus, we observe that during this period, inequality decreased in both countries. Mexico presented a 0.04 point decrease, going from 0.50 in 2000 to 0.46 in 2018, while Japan presented a 0.1 points decrease, going from 0.33 to 0.23 during the same period[8].

Japan ranks among the Organization for Economic Cooperation and Development (OECD) countries with a medium level of inequality, while Mexico not only has the highest inequality in this group but has persisted over the years. According to the OECD, the average annual income after tax of a family in Japan represents USD 26,588 while in Mexico it reached the sum of USD 13,965 (USD)[9] in 2020.

According to the OECD statistics, in the middle of the first decade of the 21st century among the 30 member countries of the organization, Mexico recorded the highest rate of relative poverty of 18.5 percent, followed by Turkey 17.5 percent and the United States 17 percent, while Japan occupied the fourth place with 15 percent (Nippon 2014).

Global Gender Gap Index, and underlying non-market gender asymmetries and symmetries

There are gender gaps in both Mexico and Japan, and differences between them. These gender gaps not only condition the economic, political, and social development of the countries but also indicate deficiencies in public policies to achieve the SDGs. The asymmetries between a developed country, such as Japan, and an underdeveloped country were observed through macroeconomic indicators. The Gini index showed the poor distribution of income in Mexico in relation to Japan. First we present the gender gaps are revealed by the Global Gender Gap Index, developed by the World Economic Forum (WEF), comparing Mexico and Japan, and then data on

Table 1. Mexico and Japan: Global Gender Gap Index 2006–2018.

Years	Mexico ranking	Japan ranking	Total average Mexico	Total average Japan
2006	75	79	0.65	0.64
2007	93	91	0.64	0.65
2008	97	98	0.64	0.64
2009	98	101	0.65	0.64
2010	91	94	0.66	0.65
2011	89	98	0.66	0.65
2012	84	101	0.67	0.65
2013	68	105	0.69	0.65
2014	80	104	0.69	0.66
2015	71	101	0.70	0.67
2016	66	111	0.70	0.66
2017	81	114	0.69	0.66
2018	50	110	0.72	0.66

Source: Own elaboration whit data from The Global Gender Gap Index. Available in: https://bit.ly/34gP4q0.

a key factor underlying these gaps: the size and gender distribution of unpaid care and domestic work in families.

Global Gender Gap Index

For 2006, out of 153 countries, the Global Gender Gap Index placed Mexico at the 75th position and Japan at 80th, with 0.646 and 0.645 scores, respectively. Both nations were then in a pretty similar situation, but they grew farther apart from each other since Mexico climbed from 68th place in 2013 to 50th place in 2018, and Japan fell from 105th to 110th during the same period.

Mexico enjoyed significant progress from 2009 onwards with constant increase in the value of the Global Gender Gap Index[10] until the end of the entire period between 2006 and 2018. Japan recorded an average of 0.659 with small increases until 2015, followed by a fall and then a quite small recovery in the last three years (Table 1). These changes are observable through the places each country has had in the world ranking. According to the latest Global Gender Gap Index, the 2020 data indicates a more significant gap in the ranking as Japan fell to 121st place with a score of 0.652 (WEF 2020) and Mexico climbed to 25th place with a 0.754 score.

Mexico's improvement in the rankings may be attributed to its enhancement in the Political Empowerment sub-index, which presented a value of 0.355 for Mexico, and 0.081 for Japan in 2020. This improvement resulted from adopting policies that introduced equal quotas of men and women in election candidates put forward by political parties, and in the legislature and government positions. Political Empowerment, which is still a pending issue in Japan, needs to be ensured to improve its gender equality outcomes. In 2006, Japan ranked in 83rd place with a 0.067 score in the Political Empowerment sub-index, and Mexico at 45th place with a 0.133 score. Japan fell to 144th place with a 0.049 score, and Mexico reached 14th place with a 0.468 score in 2020 (WEF 2020).

Education and health indicators

According to the Global Gender Gap Index (GGGI), the gender gaps in education[11] and health resulted in a similar ranking for both Mexico and Japan in 2018; but the levels of women's education and health are very different. For instance, compared to Japan, effective access to health services remains insufficient in Mexico. In the field of education, the proportion of the female population enrolled in basic and university education is greater in Japan. In Mexico, only one-sixth of the women who had enrolled in basic education also enrolled in university education. Due to high rates of inequality and poverty in developing countries, such as Mexico, girls and women are unable to continue studying and remain relegated to unpaid domestic and care work.

In 2012, in Japan 98.1 percent of female students and 97.8 percent of male students were able to reach senior high school. Of those, 55.6 percent of men and 45.8 percent of women continued with undergraduate studies, although 10 percent of these female graduates attended junior college" (Japanese Ministry of Education, Culture, Sports and Technology (MEXT) 2012; Japan Gender Equality Bureau 2014). However, in Japan the proportion of female researchers[12] was 14.6 percent according to data from the Japanese Ministry of Education, Culture, Sports, and Technology (MEXT) and the Japan Gender Equality Bureau.

In Mexico, only 36 percent of the National System of Researchers (SNI)[13] are women. The national literacy rate for women is 99.2 percent, but "... the degree of absorption in higher education incorporates 71 out of every 100 men and 66 out of every 100 women. Men have greater opportunities to enter higher education" according to the National Institute for Women (Instituto Nacional de las Mujeres (INMUJERES) 2018, 102).

The reasons for Japanese and Mexican women to abandon their jobs are mostly related to family, double shifts, the responsibility of the home, and, especially, the "decision to have children" (Zabludovsky, 2007). In Mexico, in addition, factors such as adolescent pregnancy and child marriages significantly impact women's professional career.

For the Education Attainment and Health and Survival sub-indexes, in 2018 both countries recorded similar values since the gender gaps are very similar despite the evident difference in the level of provision of these services in the two countries. One of the main drawbacks of this index is that it does not provide separate data by health and education as to why the Education Attainment and Health and Survival sub-indexes attain similar values for both Mexico and Japan.

Underlying non-market gender asymmetries and symmetries

A key element that underpins gender gaps in what refers to the distribution of employment and wages revealed by the Index is the percentage of unpaid care and domestic work, that is mainly carried out by women.

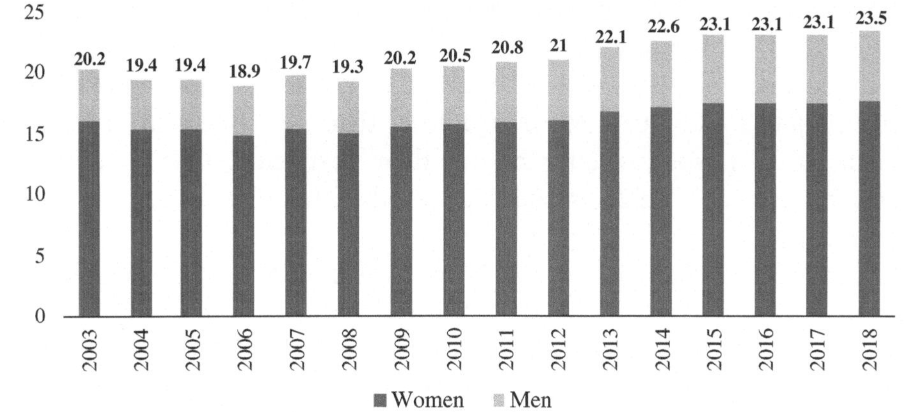

Figure 1. Mexico. Unpaid care and domestic work in relation to GDP 2003–2018. *Source:* Own elaboration with data from INEGI. Available in:https://bit.ly/2l6cupq.

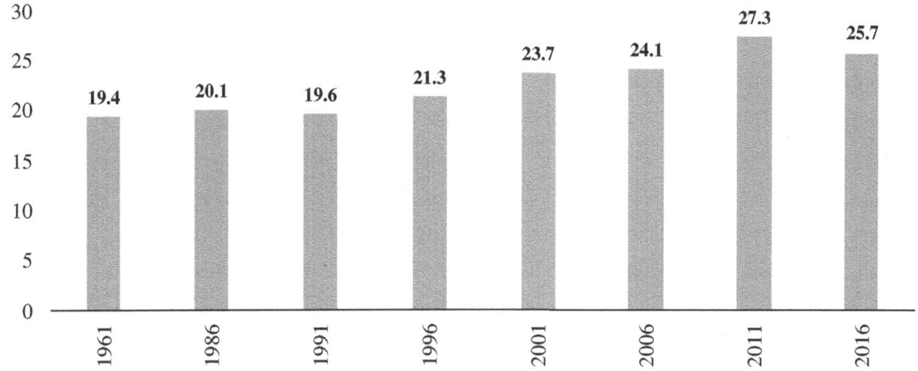

Figure 2. Japan: unpaid care and domestic work in relation to GDP (%) 1961–2016. *Source:* Own elaboration with data from Economic and Social Research Institute, Cabinet Office Regional and Specific Accounts Division, National Accounts Department. Available in:https://bit.ly/3kaGxKe.

Unpaid care and domestic work is large in relation to GDP and generates economic benefits for nations (Figures 1 and 2). In the case of Mexico, unpaid care and domestic work represents 23.5 percent of the GDP for 2018. In the case of Japan the situation is similar: unpaid care and domestic work amounted to 25.7 percent, more than a quarter of the 2016 GDP.

Average unpaid working hours per day for women in Mexico amounted to 6.2 for 2016, with 29 percent of the female EAP[14] employed in part-time jobs (WEF 2016). Several publications as CEPAL and INEGI found that 20 percent of adult Mexican women who attended university do not use their knowledge in some paid job. If doing housework were a free choice, an equivalent number of men with a university education would only do housework, but the proportion is 0.2 percent. Therefore, it is a great wasted potential that constitutes part of the so-called gender bonus (CEPAL 2019; INEGI 2015). In Japan, average unpaid working hours per day for women amounted to 5 for 2016, with 33 percent of the female EAP employed in part-time jobs (WEF 2016, 10). Koshi notes that "... 60 percent of Japanese women stopped working after having their first child. One of the main causes of this labor exile is the state of the childcare system in Japan" (Koshi 2015).

In Japanese families, it is women who are mostly in charge of household activities, which include the care and upbringing of children. "The tendency for women to quit their jobs at the time of marriage or childbirth had once served as a screening system for most companies, in that the most "desirable" women workers were those who continued to work without any interruptions from the time of their graduation" (Ueno 1989, 6).

The information compiled by the Ministry of Health, Labor, and Welfare shows that 19,895 children were waiting to enter authorized daycare centers in Japan as of April 1, 2018. "Social norms in Japan appoint women to the role of the primary, if not sole, provider of services in the family. At first sight, equality appears to have been achieved by the strategy of disregarding gender. However, for as long as the public sphere defines itself in terms of masculinity, women who become producers or soldiers have to resign themselves to being second-class workers or soldiers. Otherwise, all that awaits them is a choice between denying their femaleness or seeking to become male clones. This means acquiring a double burden and doing their best to maintain their womanly role while being reduced to an auxiliary labor force. Both traps are all too familiar within modern feminism" (Ueno 2004, 63. As cited in Mackie 2013, 4).

The unpaid and paid care sectors are crucial for the creation of public policies that look to improve gender equity in both countries, and governments should not neglect them. It is necessary to close the gender gap in the unpaid care and domestic activities, since their distribution is biased, leaving most of the unpaid care and domestic work only to women.

Violence against women is another major non-market factor underlying gender gaps. 63 percent of women over 15 years of age in Mexico have been victims of gender violence, and many of these crimes remain unreported (OECD, 2020). In the Japanese case, "When Japan improved its system for reporting and investigating domestic violence in 2011, the number of cases reported increased dramatically. An additional 46.3 percent surge after that change. In Japan, 26 percent of women were punched, kicked, or shoved, with another 14 percent forced to have sex. 18 percent of Japanese women also suffer psychological abuse, so longer-term counseling and mental health treatment are necessary" (The Japan Times 2013).

Table 2. Mexico and Japan: average wages by gender (thousands of dollars) 2005–2017.

	Japan		Mexico	
Year	Men	Women	Men	Women
2005	48.1	32.3	18.8	15.7
2006	47.8	32	19	15.5
2007	47.4	32.4	18.4	16.1
2008	47.1	32.6	19.3	15
2009	46	33	18.8	15.7
2010	46.9	33.4	17.2	15.2
2011	47.6	34.6	17.2	15.5
2012	46.5	34.2	17.2	14.9
2013	46.5	34.2	17.4	14.7
2014	45.5	33.7	17.6	14.4
2015	45.4	33.8	17.7	14.8
2016	46	34.7	17.6	14.7
2017	46.2	34.9	17.1	15.2
Average	46.7	33.5	17.9	15.2

Source: Own elaboration with OECD data. Aviable in: http://bit.ly/35AvvsY. *Note*: the values were calculated from the series "Average Annual Wages" and "Gender Wage Gap" reported by the OECD, at 2018 prices.

Gender gaps in wages and employment

There was a decrease in average wages in Mexico: for men, a reduction from 18.8 to 17.1 thousand dollars and, for women, from 15.7 to 15.2 thousand dollars for the period 2005—2017. In Japan, the average wage for men went down from 48.1 to 46.2 thousand dollars, whereas for women it increased from 32.3 to 34.9 thousand dollars between 2005 and 2017.

Table 2 below shows the average wages in Mexico and Japan 2005–2017. There is a wage gap in levels of earnings between men and women in both countries, larger in Japan than in Mexico. On average the wage gap in Japan was 13.2 thousand dollars. Despite the drop in wages between men and women, in Mexico the wage gap was 2.7 thousand dollars.

The following Table 3 shows the women's median earnings as a percentage of men's median earnings in Japan and Mexico. By 2005, women in Japan received 67.2 percent of what men received; in Mexico, women earned 83.3 percent. In Japan, women increased their earnings to 75.5 percent of men's earnings in 2017, while the wage gap decreased to 24.5 percent compared to 2005. In Mexico, women received 88.9 percent of men's wages in 2017 and the wage gap decreased to 11.1 percent. Despite the fact that the wage gap between men and women decreased in both countries, the wage gender gap in Japan is double than that in Mexico. The gender wage gap as defined by the OECD was 32.8 percent in Japan, and 16.6 percent in Mexico in 2018[15].

On average in APEC countries during 2000–2018 (Table 4), 35.8 percent of women workers worked part-time and 20.7 percent of men: a difference of 15 percentage points between women and men[16]. Before the GFC, female part-time employment was around 40 percent of female employment, and men's was 22 percent. After the crisis, part-time employment for

Table 3. Mexico and Japan: wage proportion (%) 2005–2017.

Year	Japan	Mexico
2005	67.2	83.3
2006	67	81.4
2007	68.3	87.5
2008	69.3	77.8
2009	71.7	83.3
2010	71.3	88.4
2011	72.6	90
2012	73.5	86.4
2013	73.4	84.6
2014	74.1	81.7
2015	74.3	83.3
2016	75.4	83.5
2017	75.5	88.9
Average	71.8	84.6

Source: Own elaboration with OECD data. Available in: http://bit.ly/35AvvsY.

Table 4. Part-time employment for APEC countries by gender (%), 2000–2018.

	APEC average	
Year	Women	Men
2000	38.5	20.2
2001	39.6	21.6
2002	39.4	22.1
2003	39.8	22.5
2004	39.2	21.9
2005	38.0	21.0
2006	37.6	22.4
2007	39.5	22.8
2008	39.0	22.8
2009	33.2	20.2
2010	33.3	19.7
2011	32.5	19.8
2012	33.6	19.9
2013	33.4	20.1
2014	31.3	18.7
2015	31.9	18.3
2016	30.4	18.4
2017	34.7	20.5
2018	35.9	21.0
Period average	35.8	20.7

Source: Own elaboration with data from the World Bank, available at http://bit.ly/2Hy2yBV

women and men fell to about 32 and 20 percent, respectively. The latter is explained by the need to increase family income by extending the workday. This trend prevailed during 2009–2016; the following year, part-time employment as a share of employment again approached average values.

The average part-time work for women as a share of women's employment in APEC was 31.3 percent and, for Japan and Mexico, the averages were 49.8 and 34.4 percent, respectively, in 2014[17]. The average part-time work for men as a share of men's employment in Japan and Mexico were 20.5 and 18.3 percent, while the part-time work gaps were 29.3 percentage points for Japan and 16.2 percentage points for Mexico (World Bank 2020).

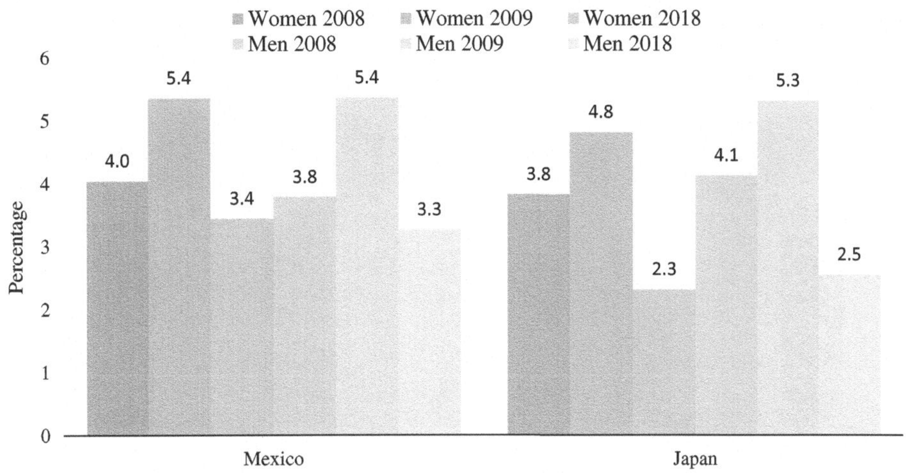

Figure 3. Mexico and Japan: unemployment rate by gender 2008–2018. *Source:* Own elaboration with data from the World Bank. Available in: https://bit.ly/3kEq2qe.

The wage gap in Mexico, and the part-time work gap was smaller, while there was an observable tendency in Japan for women to be partially employed. One explanation for this phenomenon is the family structure that prevents women from participating in full-time work and the lack of public policies that lead to greater inclusion of women in the labor market. However, the greater participation of women in full-time work in Mexico than in Japan does not necessarily imply the implementation of more beneficial public policies for women. Many women in Mexico work in the informal economy, but that is unregistered for part-time employment, so the statistical data is biased.

Unemployment and distribution of employment by economic sectors

There was an increase in the unemployment rate of women and men between 2008 and 2009 (Figure 3) as a consequence of the GFC. The unemployment rate amongst women in Mexico increased by 1.4 percentage points, with unemployment growing by 32.5 percent in just one year. The increase in the unemployment rate for men was 1.6 percentage points and there was a 41.5 percent increase in unemployment growth rate[18].

The unemployment rate for women in Japan increased by 1 percentage point between 2008 and 2009, which means an unemployment growth rate of 25.7 percent. The unemployment rate for men increased by 1.2 percentage points, representing a 28.6 percent growth rate in unemployment. The 2018 data shows a decrease in unemployment, below the existing rates before the GFC for Japan, as observed for Mexico, to 2.3 percent for women and 2.5 percent for men, which translates into a cumulative decrease in the unemployment growth rate by 52 percent for both genders since 2009 (Figure 3).

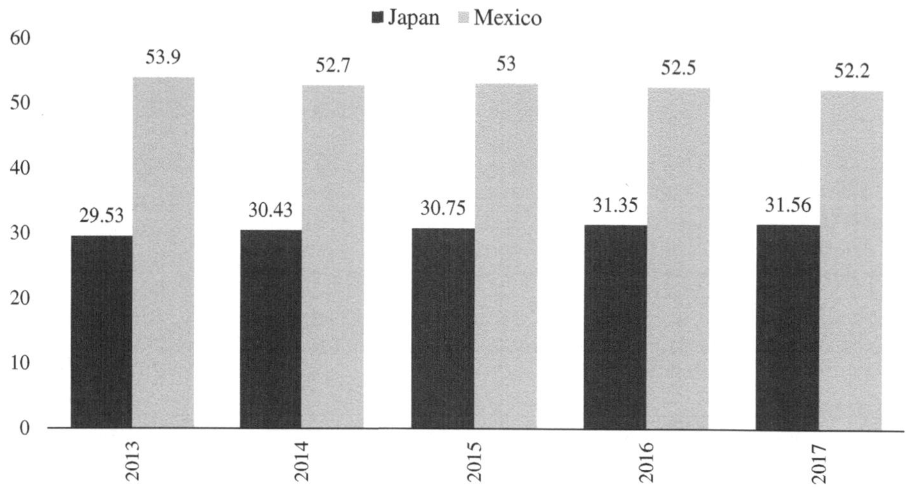

Figure 4. Mexico and Japan: informal employment (%) 2013–2017. *Source*: Own elaboration with data from the Statistisc Bureau of Japan and ILOSTAT. Available in: https://bit.ly/2IQkM5fy and https://bit.ly/37vWcRI.

In Japan, 68 percent of the economically active population is employed in the formal sector, while in Mexico only 48 percent. Income inequality is broadly related to the distribution of employment and in Mexico most employment is in the informal sector[19]. Figures 4 and 5 show this data in greater detail.

The distribution of male and female employment by productive sector changed somewhat after the GFC (Figure 6). The data refer to the shares of each sector in male and female total employment. The proportion of women's employment in the Mexican agricultural sector decreased and increased in the services sector. Their employment in the industrial sector remained unchanged. The industrial sector accounted for a larger share of men's employment, with an increase of around 1 percent compared to the agriculture and services sectors where the share of men's employment decreased by 0.6 and 0.3 percent, respectively. The proportion of women's employment accounted for by the agricultural and industrial sectors of Japan decreased, but there was an increase of 3.8 percent in the share of women's employment accounted for by the services sector. The employed male population experienced a similar situation since there was a decrease in the share of their employment accounted for by the agricultural and industrial sectors and a 2.7 percent increase in the share of their employment accounted for by the services sector.

Financial and digital inclusion

Financial and digital inclusion is one of the Seven Drivers of Women's Economic Empowerment[20] and it is a key issue to reduce gender gaps.

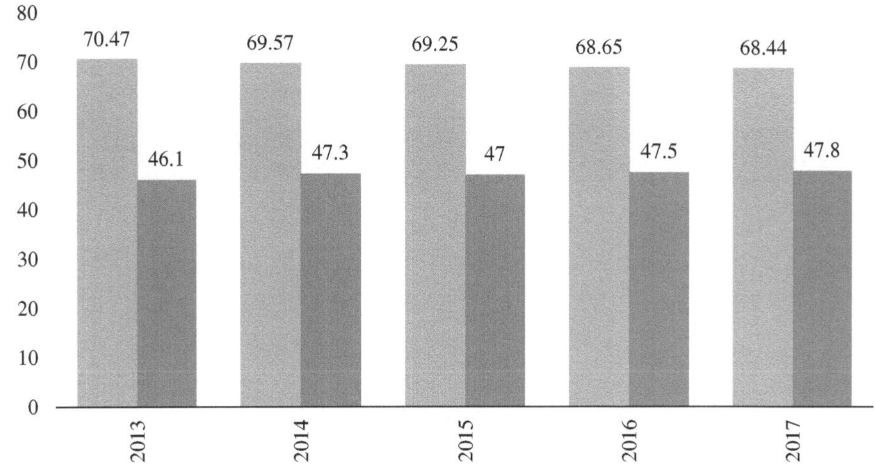

Figure 5. Mexico and Japan: formal employment (%) 2013–2017. *Source*: Own elaboration with data from Statistisc Bureau of Japan and ILOSTAT. Available in: https://bit.ly/2lQkM5f and https://bit.ly/37vWcRl.

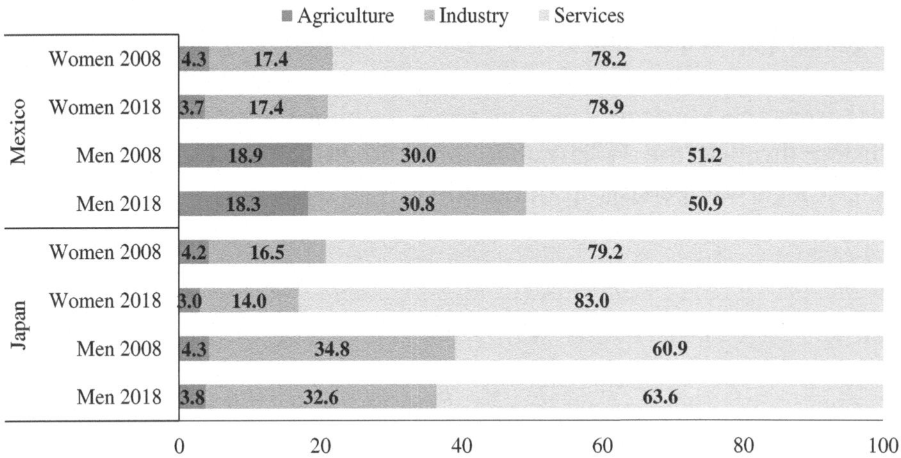

Figure 6. Mexico and Japan: employment distribution by sector and gender 2008–2018. *Source*: Own elaboration with data from the International Labor Organization.

The access to "… digital technology innovations and applications have the potencial to accelerate women's economic empowerment" (UNHLP 2017, 10). Access to digital financial services is very relevant in the current context of COVID-19, and also in looking to post COVID recovery. Table 5 shows financial and digital inclusion comparing Mexico and Japan to the other APEC countries. Japan stands out as one of the countries with the highest digital access to financial services, 98.1 percent of women and 98.5 percent of men, with a very small 0.4 percent gender gap.

On the other side, Mexico stands out with the lowest inclusion since only 50 percent of its population has access to digital financial services.

Table 5. APEC countries, access to financial services (% of population +15 years), 2017.

Country	Women	Men
Canada	99.9	99.6
New Zealand	99.3	99.0
Australia	99.2	99.9
Japan	98.1	98.5
Singapore	96.3	99.7
Hong Kong	94.7	96.0
South Korea	94.7	95.0
U.S	92.7	93.6
Malaysia	82.5	87.9
Thailand	79.8	83.7
China	76.4	84.0
Russia	76.1	75.3
Chile	71.3	77.8
Indonesia	51.4	46.2
Philippines	38.9	30.0
Peru	34.4	51.0
Mexico	33.3	41.1
Vietnam	30.4	31.2

Note: there is no data for Brunei Darussalam and Papau New Guinea. *Source*: Own elaboration with data from the World Bank, available at http://bit.ly/2Hy2yBV.

The gender gap is also substantial with only 33 percent of women included, compared to 41.1 percent of men; a gap of 7.8 percent. Regardless of the efforts from the Mexican Government in seeking the promotion of greater inclusion through the Financial Reform of 2014, the gap in digital and financial inclusion persists in the country.

Conclusions

Japan is a developed country with a per capita income that ranks 5th, and Mexico, an underdeveloped country, ranked 13th among APECs countries. However, their rankings are reversed on the Global Gender Gap Index, with Mexico ranked 14th and Japan 144th.This paper has investigated the similarities and differences between Japan and Mexico in their gender gaps. This research concludes that there is no necessary correlation between the development level of an economy and its gender gaps. Based on economic participation and opportunity, educational attainment, health and survival, and political empowerment, the Global Gender Gap Index reveals gaps that have to be addressed by public policies seeking to reduce gender gaps.

Incorporating the gender dimension is a key in the development of public policies to address the UN 2030 Development Agenda. To improve Women's Economic Empowerment, public policies must reduce Gender Gaps. We must not forget the "… modern nation-states are gendered, and they operate according to the principles of inclusion and exclusion (Germer, Mackie, and Wöhr, 2014). The importance of a State is the capacity to provide public goods, has been weakened by the austerity policies carried out in Mexico and a change in the monetary policies carried out by the BoJ in Japan during the last decades. It is essential to reverse them. Investment in the economy of care is essential for both Mexico and Japan. Looking to the future, digital and financial inclusion is necessary for women's self-employment and may require banking and microfinance reforms.

After a decade of the Global Financial Crisis and the COVID-19 pandemic, gender asymmetries deepened and announced a reverse in the global gender gaps as well as in macroeconomic indexes.

Notes

1. After the collapse of the bubble during the late '80s and early '90s, the financial crisis and the high NPLs and low interest rates, the BoJ induced deflation.
2. The Montevideo Strategy for the Implementation of the Regional Gender Agenda in the framework of the Sustainable Development of 2030, approved by the Economic Commission for Latin America and the Caribbean (ECLAC) members, stated during the 13th Regional Conference on Women in Latin America and the Caribbean, aims at guiding the implementation of the Gender Regional Agenda.
3. To overcome these problems, 74 measures were established in ten axes of implementation: (1) Regulatory framework, (2) institutionality, (3) participation, (4) construction and building capability, (5) financing, (6) communication, (7) technology, (8) cooperation, (9) information systems, and (10) monitoring, evaluation, and accountability (ECLAC, 2017, 21, 22).
4. The patriarchal cultural patterns in Latin America also underlie the wage gap, vocational orientation, the social organization of care and the violence perpetrated against women and girls. It is embedded in daily life. The Montevideo Strategy defines the need "… to move from a culture of privilege to one of rights and equality, dismantling the androcentric understanding of the human being and its expression in public policies, and including boys, young men and men as agents and beneficiaries of this change. It is necessary, therefore, to eliminate all types of sex-based distinction, exclusion or restriction aimed at or resulting in the denial of effective enjoyment of human rights in the political, economic, social, cultural and environmental sphere (ECLAC 2016, 17).
5. Precisely, Mexico's GDP per capita was equivalent to 21.22% compared to that of Japan in 2018.
6. APEC consists of 21 countries: Australia, Brunei Darussalam, Canada, Chile, China, Hong Kong, Indonesia, Japan, Malaysia, Mexico, New Zealand, Papua New Guinea, Peru, Philippines, Russia, Singapore, South Korea, Thailand, Taiwan, United States, and Vietnam. Statistics available at the World Bank do not provide information for Taiwan because it is considered part of China.
7. The Gini coefficient is an indicator used to measure the inequality degree in the distribution of income between individuals or households within an economy. Its value ranges from zero to one; the higher the index, the greater the inequality in income distribution. It measures income inequality on a scale from 0 (everyone has the same income) to 100 (all income is for a single person) and in practice it is between 20 and 80 for the countries of the world.
8. Data from 2000 to 2015–16 obtained from the Organization for Economic Cooperation and Development (OECD), for 2018, obtained from and World Economic Forum (WEF).

9. Average amount of money a family earns per year, after tax. Source: http://www.oecdbetterlifeindex.org/es/topics/income-es/
10. There are three basic concepts underlying the Global Gender Gap Index of the World Economic Forum, creating the basis of the way in which the indicators were chosen, the way in which data is treated and the way in which the scale can be used. First, the index focuses on measuring gaps rather than levels. Second, it captures gaps in outcome variables rather than gaps in input variables. Third, it ranks countries according to gender equality rather than women's empowerment. The publication of the Global Gender Gap Index was developed in 2006. The value of this index is calculated by taking the average of the four sub-indexes from which it is composed: (1) Economic Participation and economic Opportunity subindex; (2) Educational Attainment subindex; (3) Health and Survival subindex; (4) Political Empowerment subindex.
11. Education attainment 0.949 and Health and survival 0.955 were the same in Japan and Mexico as it is described by The Global Gender Gap Report (World Economic Forum, 2018, 139, 185).
12. In this quotation it is not mentioned if they are only in universities or research centers in general.
13. The National System of Researchers (SNI) of Mexico was created on July 26, 1984. Its purpose is to recognize the research work in the country, through a scientific and technological competition, and thereby contribute to increasing international competitiveness in the matter and the resolution of national problems. As a prize, distinctions and economic incentives are awarded that certify the quality, productivity, significance, and impact of the work of the selected researchers.
14. The economically active population is made up of all people aged 12 and over who carried out some type of economic activity (employed population), or who actively sought to do so (open unemployed population), in the two months prior to the week of lifting the EAP. It is classified into the employed population and the open unemployed population or the active unemployed.
15. The gender wage gap is defined as the difference between median earnings of men and women relative to median earnings of men. Data refer to full-time employees on the one hand and to self-employed on the other (OCDE 2018).
16. World Bank, database 2019.
17. 2014 was considered as the year with the highest number of countries with information, only missing China and Papua New Guinea.
18. It is important to be clear about the difference between the unemployment rate and the unemployment growth rate. The first refers to the percentage of the population that is unemployed with respect to the economically active population, while the second refers to the variations in unemployment from one year to another.
19. Informal employment refers primarily to employment in enterprises that lack registration and social security coverage for their employees (OECD 2009). It also refers to self-employment and precarious employment in formal enterprises. A distinctive feature of this type of employment is the lack of social coverage and other related benefits applicable to formal employment. (The World Bank 2014, 6)
20. The Seven primary drivers of women's economic empowerment are: (1) Tackling adverse norms and promoting positive role models; (2) Ensuring legal protection and reforming discriminatory laws and regulations; (3) Recognizing and redistributing unpaid word and care, (4) Building assets – Digital, financial and property; (5) changing business culture and practice; (6) Improving public sector practices in employment and procurement; (7) Strengthening visibility, collective voice and representation (UNHLP 2017, 4).

Acknowledgment

This work is the result of the statistical support provided by Jairo Cisneros, Daniel Mirón and Adheli Galindo, scholarship holders from CONACYT, Yasmín Águila and Díaz from the project "Women, Social Reproduction, Public Budgets and Prospects for Socioeconomic Integration Mexico-Central America" (PAPIIT IN304420), UNAM General Department of Academic Staff Affairs.

ORCID

Alicia Girón http://orcid.org/0000-0002-7513-3719

References

CEPAL. 2010. "Género, trabajo remunerado y no remunerado: eslabones en la discriminación y la desigualdad. Panorama Social de América Latina 2009." Santiago de Chile: CEPAL. https://bit.ly/3pQDaeT.

ECLAC. 2016. "Montevideo Strategy for Implementation of the Regional Gender Agenda within the Sustainable Development Framework by 2030." https://bit.ly/2XjCa6x.

ECLAC. 2017. "Montevideo Strategy for Implementation of the Regional Gender Agenda within the Sustainable Development Framework by 2030". Accessed November 10, 2020. https://bit.ly/3jCLHQn

Germer, A., V. Mackie, and U. Wöhr (Eds.). 2014. *Gender, Nation and State in Modern Japan.* 1st ed. London and New York: Routledge.

Groysberg, B., M. Yamazaki, N. Sato, and D. Lane. 2017. "Womenomics in Japan". Harvard Business School Case 417-002. Retrieved November 9, 2019, from: https://s.hbr.org/2S60V4E.

INEGI. 2015. "Encuesta Intercensal 2015." Encuesta en hogares. https://bit.ly/3cIfPsa.

INMUJERES. 2018. "Mujeres y Hombres en México 2018." Retrieved November 8, 2019, from: http://bit.ly/2sGq0IK.

Instituto Nacional de Estadística y Geografía. 2018. "Cuenta Satélite del Trabajo no remunerado de los hogares de México, 2017." Retrieved November 24, 2019, from: http://bit.ly/34Bn65a

Japan Gender Equality Bureau. 2014. "Education and Research Fields." Retrieved November 14, 2019, from: http://bit.ly/2PDYkgV.

Japan Gender Equality Bureau. 2014. "White Paper on Gender Equality 2013". *Statistical Topic* (Japanese). Retrieved November 4, 2019, from: http://bit.ly/35DhUiy.

Japanese Ministry of Education. Culture, Sports and Technology (MEXT). 2012. "Gender Equality". Retrieved November 24 2019 from: http://bit.ly/36NJfih.

Koshi, N. 2015. "¿Cómo podemos mejorar la igualdad de género en Japón?" [on line]. World Economic Forum. Retrieved November 24, 2019, from: http://bit.ly/38MTMw9.

Mackie, V. C. 2013. "Feminism and the Nation-State in Japan." *Electronic Journal of Contemporary Japanese Studies* 12 (3):1–6. http://bit.ly/34C4hiz.

Nippon. 2014. "La pobreza sigue creciendo en Japón." Accessed November 24, 2019. http://bit.ly/2Z77ENo.

OECD. 2009. "Is Informal Normal? Towards More and Better Jobs in Developing Countries." https://www.oecd.org/development/risinginformalemploymentwillincrease-poverty.htm.

OCDE. 2018. "Mujeres en México, el talento olvidado." Retrieved November 24, 2019, from: http://bit.ly/2S87pjq.

OECD. 2020. "Gender Wage Gap." https://bit.ly/35jgQlQ.

The Japan Times. 2013. "Violence against Women." Retrieved November 5, 2020, from: https://bit.ly/38jawx3.

The World Bank. 2014. "Informal Economy and the World Bank." https://bit.ly/2MxmfPK.

Ueno, C. 1989. "Women's Labor under Patriarchal Capitalism in the Eighties." *Review of Japanese Culture and Society* 3 (1):1–6. Retrieved November 24 2019 from: http://bit.ly/36Qudsk.

Ueno, C. 2004. *Nationalism and Gender*, translated by Beverley Yamamoto. Melbourne: Trans Pacific Press.

Ueno, C. 1998. "The Declining Birthrate: Whose Problem?" *Review of Population and Social Policy* 7:103–128. http://bit.ly/2PZozx3.

UNHLP. 2017. "Leave No One Behind, Taking Action for Transformational Change on Women's Economic Empowerment, Secretariat, UN Secretary-General's High-Level Panel on Women's Economic Empowerment."

Westelius, N. 2020. "Twenty Years of Unconventional Monetary Policies: Lessons and Way forward for the Bank of Japan." International Monetary Fund, Working Paper 226. https://bit.ly/38kI9yh.

World Bank. 2020. "World Development Indicators." http://bit.ly/2Hy2yBV.

World Economic Forum. 2016. "Closing the Economic Gender Gap: Learning from the Gender Parity Task Forces." Retrieved November 7, 2019, from: http://bit.ly/35F5sik.

World Economic Forum. 2018. "The Global Gender Gap Report 2018." Accessed November 10, 2020. https://bit.ly/3tCDoIV

World Economic Forum. 2020. "The Global Gender Gap Report 2020." Retrieved December 28, 2020, from: https://bit.ly/39iEtfy.

Zabludovsky, G. 2007. "Las mujeres en México: trabajo, educación superior y esferas de poder." Retrieved November 14, 2019, from: http://bit.ly/2M9bKiq

Intersections of gender and class in the distribution of income

Diane Elson

ABSTRACT
This article considers the intersection of gender and class in the distribution of income. The first section applies a gender lens to reread Piketty's *Capital in the Twenty-First Century*, showing how the analysis would be different if capitalism were recognized as not only patrimonial but also patriarchal. The second section discusses an OECD study that claimed, "More women in paid work means less income inequality," taking into account unpaid work as well as paid work. The third section discusses the claim that rising female labor force participation is associated with a rise in inequality between capital and labor. The final section considers strategies to reduce both gender inequality and class inequality.

Introduction

In the last decade, economic inequality has come to the forefront of research by economists in academic institutions, NGOs, and international organizations. A book examining trends in the concentration of income and wealth in the century since 1910 in the hands of the top 1 percent of people in the United States, the United Kingdom, France, Germany, and Japan became an international bestseller (Piketty 2014). In the period from the early 1980s to around 2010, Piketty showed that inequality intensified—especially in the United States, where the top percentile's share of national income rose to nearly 20 percent, compared to around 14 percent in the United Kingdom, around 9 percent in France and Japan, and 11 percent in Germany (Piketty 2014: 316–317).

In a global study of recent experience in distribution of the fruits of economic growth, Oxfam showed that, although all income groups experienced positive growth in their real income between 1988 and 2011, the incomes of the poorest 10 percent of people increased by $65, equivalent to less than $3 extra a year, whereas the incomes of the richest 1 percent increased

182 times as much, by $11,800 (Oxfam 2017). At the same time, the functional distribution of income changed in favor of capital. Drawing on ILO (2013) and Stockhammer (2013), the United Nations Development Program (UNDP) reported that in a group of 16 developed countries for which data were available, the labor share of national income declined from about 75 percent in the mid-1970s to 65 percent in the mid-2000s; and in a group of 16 developing and emerging economies for which data were available, average labor shares declined from around 62 percent of gross domestic product (GDP) in the early 1990s to 58 percent in the mid-2000s (UNDP 2015).

Evidence of growing inequality in the distribution of income between rich and poor people and between capital and labor has not only been produced by heterodox economists but also highlighted by mainstream organizations such as IMF and OECD in their reports. For instance, the IMF highlighted trends in income inequality between households in Group of 20 (G20) countries in a Policy Note to G20 governments, drawing attention to the disproportionately large share of income that has accrued to the top 1 percent of the income distribution (IMF 2017). In G20 countries, the combined labor share of low- and middle-skilled labor fell by more than 10 percentage points from 1995 to 2009, whereas that for highly skilled labor rose by more than 5 percentage points in "emerging G20" countries and by 10 percentage points in "advanced G20" countries (IMF 2017).

The focus on distribution of income and wealth inequality allows class to make some reappearance in economic discourse, even though such a focus does not probe the roots of class inequality in the capitalist system of production[1]. However, none of the measures of income and wealth distribution commonly used by economists explicitly address the gender dimension of economic inequality. Measures of inequality in income and wealth between "people" are actually measures of inequality between households, or between tax units (which may be individuals or couples)[2]. Inequality within households (or tax units) is ignored. The functional distribution measures income inequality between factors of production: labor (sometimes differentiated by skill levels[3]) and capital. When economists consider drivers of inequality, they mainly focus on processes of technical change, globalization, diverging returns to different skills, structures of property rights and inheritance, and the ability of the rich to capture economic policy making and shape it to serve their interests. On the whole, they do not situate economic inequality between people in the context of intersecting inequalities of gender, race/ethnicity, and location that shape the access that different people have to income and wealth.

This article considers the intersection of gender and class in the distribution of income and, to some extent, wealth. Gender is understood not as an innate personal characteristic but as an unequal structure of social power that is always intertwined with other unequal structures of social power, such as class. A person's gender position shapes how he or she experiences class, and his or her class position shapes how he or she experiences gender (Beneria and Sen 1982). Structures of gender inequality intersect with income inequality, shaping inequality outcomes, with implications for men as well as for women. To fully understand economic inequality, we need to recognize that economies (and economic policies) are not gender neutral but have gender biases built into them (Elson 1991, 1999). Economies are gendered structures in which the public and private sectors depend on the process of social reproduction of people in the domestic sector of families and communities, through unpaid care and domestic work (Elson 1998)[4], a process not visible in most economy-wide analyses, but made visible in feminist analysis (Cagatay, Elson, and Grown 1995, 2000; Heintz 2019).

Trends in inequality between women and men in the labor market are not necessarily the same as trends in inequality between households and between labor and capital. For instance, UNDP (2015) provided an analysis of global trends in the period 1990–2010 of gender gaps in four labor market variables: employment-to-population ratios, 15 years and older; unemployment rates; wages; and shares of females and males employed in the industrial sector. It found that there has been a narrowing of the global mean gender gap in employment to population ratio; gender gap in unemployment rates fell in Asia but not in other regions; some progress—but very slow—in reducing the gender wage gap in OECD countries and fast-growing Asian economies; and defeminization of industrial sectors in many middle-income countries.

The first section of this article applies a gender lens to reread Piketty's *Capital in the Twenty-First Century,* showing how the analysis would be different if capitalism were recognized as not only patrimonial but also patriarchal. The second discusses the interaction of income inequality between households and gender inequality in labor markets, taking into account that some dimensions of gender inequality in labor markets have been falling. Research by the OECD on the distribution of income between households has found that rising female labor force participation has served to reduce the rise in inequality below what it would otherwise have been (OECD 2015). I ask whether the OECD conclusion that, "More women in paid work means less income inequality," tells the whole story. The third section discusses some academic research on the distribution of income between labor and capital that finds that rising female labor force participation is associated with a rise in inequality between capital and labor (Finnoff and Jayadev 2006; Guschanski and Onaran 2017; Braunstein

2019). The final section considers strategies to reduce both gender inequality and class inequality.

Patrimonialism without patriarchy

Piketty's global bestseller on rising economic inequality characterizes capitalism as a patrimonial system, in which inheritance is a key driver of wealth inequalities, although inequality in earnings is also important. "In all societies, there are two main ways of accumulating wealth: through work and through inheritance" (Piketty 2014, 379). Although theft and pillage are mentioned in footnotes as "not totally without historical significance," Piketty paid little attention to imperialism. His main concern was to displace ideas of "meritocratic" capitalism by showing that in the rich countries, inherited wealth was important in 18th and 19th centuries, declined in period from 1914 to 1970, and is once again increasing in importance. He did this in magnificent style, using easy-to-read charts that have captured public imagination.

Patrimonialism is not seen as gendered, even though many of the examples Piketty discussed from 19th-century novels show that patrimony was patriarchal: Women had fewer inheritance rights, and men controlled the property of their wives, who did not have their own earnings. Patriarchy today in the rich countries is more subtle and is not rooted in lack of legal rights but in the persistence of systems of social reproduction that assign the main responsibility for unpaid care and domestic work to women; and in the persistence of social norms about what is appropriate work for women and men, which confine the majority of women to low-pay, low-status occupations.

Piketty paid little attention to gender. He did note that, "in most countries … women are in fact significantly overrepresented in the bottom 50 percent of earners" (2014: 256) and that these were predominantly less skilled industrial workers in the 1920–1980 period and subsequently mainly restaurant and shop workers (2014: 279–80), but he did not see this as an outcome of a gendered labor market. Rather, he suggested that the earnings of low-income workers could be explained in terms of marginal productivity theory because their work—for instance, that of assembly line workers or fast food servers—is replicable (2014: 330–331). This is not the case, he argued, for top managers, and their salaries cannot be explained in terms of marginal productivity because their job functions are "unique" (i.e., top managers are not interchangeable in the way that assembly line workers or fast food servers are interchangeable). Piketty noted that the salaries of those he calls "supermanagers," such as CEOs, are set by corporate compensation committees, leaving considerable scope for social norms to shape their pay (2014: 332). These social norms have evolved to support extremely high pay packages, especially in the United States and the United Kingdom after 1970, and to a lesser extent in Western Europe in the 1980s and 1990s. This is, argued Piketty, a key driver of the increasing inequality of labor incomes, although he did not have much to say about what shapes these social norms.

An approach to the labor market that starts from the perception that the labor market is a gendered institution (Elson 1998) challenges Piketty's assumption that the earnings of low-income workers are determined by their marginal productivity, seeing all earnings as shaped by institutions and social norms as well as technology. For instance, a key difference between low-income workers and supermanagers is that the earnings of the former are set by people who have more power than them and who are different from them, whereas the earnings of the supermanagers are set by their peers.

Perrons (2014) explored these issues by focusing on a group of low-income workers that Piketty did not mention: paid care workers. This is not a small group; paid care employment is as large as construction employment in many OECD countries (ITUC/WBG 2016). The pay of care workers is low, but care jobs are not mechanically replicable and workers are not interchangeable from the point of view of those receiving care. The continuity of a personal relation between carer and the person being cared for is a key factor in determining the quality of care (Himmelweit 2007). This means it is difficult to increase the productivity of a care worker by requiring him or her to look after more people at one time or by speeding up the care so that it is completed more quickly, without destroying the quality of care. Perrons (2014) pointed to the similarity between care workers and members of a string quartet, drawing on the famous example used by Baumol (1967). Just as doubling the speed at which the members of the quartet play, or reducing the quartet to a trio, worsens the performance of the music, the same is true of the performance of care.

As Perrons (2014) argued, the low pay of care workers can only be understood in terms of the way this work is gendered. It is seen as work women are "naturally" suited for, as they do similar work (although unpaid) for their families and communities; and as not requiring much formal training, and therefore "low skilled." In fact, it requires many tacit skills that women have acquired through their socialization at home and at school. But formal entry requirements are low in most countries, and it is open to women who have the least bargaining power (including ethnic minority women and migrant women) and the fewest alternative earning opportunities. Similar factors explain low pay in many other occupations in which women are concentrated.

Piketty (2014) showed that even more important than inequality in earnings is inequality in the ownership of wealth and in income from wealth. He showed that the reduction in equality in ownership of wealth and income from wealth in the leading rich countries "was the only reason why total income inequality diminished in the first half of the twentieth century" (2014: 336). Since then inequality in wealth and income from wealth has increased and "inherited wealth comes as close to being decisive at the beginning of the twenty-first century as it was in the age of Balzac" in 19th-century France (2014: 22).

Piketty's explanation for this has proved to be the most controversial part of his argument, subject to criticism by many heterodox economists (see, e.g., Galbraith 2014; Ghosh 2014). Here a feminist critique is developed. Piketty frames discussion of drivers of inequality in terms of the relation between rate of return on "capital" (*r*) and the rate of growth of output (*g*), arguing that in the long run *r* tends to be greater than *g*, leading through an "implacable logic" (2014: 27) to rising inequality. He claimed that *r* tends to persist on average at between 4 and 5 percent except when there is an "exogenous" shock (war, revolution, etc.), although it is not clear why this should be the case when he also conceded that *r* "depends on many technological, psychological, social and cultural factors' (2014: 361), all implied to be exogenous to economy. Unless the rate of growth of output, *g*, is higher than this, inherited wealth grows faster than output and income (2014: 26) and inequality rises; *g* depends on productivity and population increases (which are treated as exogenous), both of which are now falling in the rich countries. Piketty concluded, "Decreased growth—especially demographic growth—is thus responsible for capital's comeback' (2014: 166). His solution is a progressive global tax on capital, although he admitted that securing this would be very difficult, and his analysis indicated no intrinsic reason why the process of capital accumulation requires a fiscal process as well as a market process.

However, we can get new insights by looking at both *r* and *g* through a gender lens and examining their interaction with a part of the economy Piketty ignored, the social reproduction of labor, on an intergenerational and daily basis. Social reproduction of labor is at the core of feminist understandings of the economy, a process that is both shaped by and shapes capital accumulation (Picchio 1992; Folbre 1994; Heintz 2019). It shapes both the rate of economic growth and the rate of return on capital, but through complex, historically specific, and contradictory processes, not through "implacable logic." Recognition of this process suggests some reasons why taxation is endogenous, not exogenous, to the process of capital accumulation, although the distribution of tax obligations is a matter for social and political struggle. It also suggests that collective (as well as private) ownership of assets has proved important for capital accumulation in 20th century.

For instance, Piketty treated population growth as exogenous, but fertility decisions are not simply private, individual, exogenous choices but depend on gendered economic institutions, such as women's access to public services (reproductive health services, care services, education services) and to women's earning opportunities. Perrons (2014) pointed out that European countries with better tax-funded childcare services (and thus less requirement for parents, especially mothers, to undertake unpaid childcare) have higher fertility rates than those that do not. Moreover, labor supply is not exogenously determined by population growth. Ghosh (2014) pointed out that capitalism has always generated a supply of labor to adjust to demand, including through changing labor force participation of women. When businesses need female labor, measures are taken by both governments and businesses to draw more women into the labor market, through provision of public transport, childcare, flexible shift patterns, outsourcing to home-based producers, facilitation of migration, and so on.

However, mobilizing the labor of women to ensure a desired rate of return on capital is not without contradictions. Other things being equal, the higher the rate of return on capital can secure and keep is higher, the more the costs of social reproduction of labor can be externalized to households and communities. There is a direct effect of externalization because this weakens the bargaining power of workers, especially women workers, and an indirect effect because there is less pressure for taxation of capital to fund public services and infrastructure (such as education, health, social care, housing, clean water and sanitation, electricity, transport) to reduce the burden of unpaid work. However, other things are not equal. Women's unpaid work is not able to completely substitute for goods and services bought in the market or supplied by the state (Elson 1991), especially when the rate of return on capital comes to depend on a supply of well-educated, healthy workers. The history of capitalist development in rich countries shows that provision of tax-funded public services became critical to secure the social reproduction of the kind of labor required by 20th-century industrialization (Harvey and Geras 2018). The sphere of social reproduction of labor now encompasses not only the household and community but also public services (Pearson and Elson 2015). The extent of tax-funded public services and the distribution of tax payments vary from country to country and over time, and pressures for externalization of costs of social reproduction (and possibilities for such externalization) vary over time, but a fiscal process is intrinsic to capital accumulation. Moreover, provision of public services implies various forms of collective ownership of assets, so that the realization of returns on private assets is nevertheless implicated with some degree of collective ownership of assets. The process of capital accumulation is much more hybrid that Piketty allowed for—and, indeed, this is true of most economists, heterodox as well as mainstream.

Of course, social reproduction of labor is intrinsically a site of struggle, marked since the 1970s through offshoring and migration, which promote externalization of costs to other countries; and by marketization and privatization that intensify the externalization of their social reproduction to working-class people, especially working-class women. Not surprisingly, the share of taxes paid by rich people and businesses has tended to decline, but not to zero; and public investment and collective ownership of public assets have declined in size, but still remain indispensable. Trends in inequality cannot be adequately understood in terms of an abstract logic of whether *r* is greater than *g*. Attention needs to be paid to concrete struggles in which gender and class intersect. Policy responses do not have to be plucked exogenously from the minds of analysts but can be rooted in real contradictions of accumulation.

'More women in paid work means less income inequality': OECD analysis of interaction between class and gender

We now turn from the grand historical sweep of Piketty to a much more limited empirical study. In 2015, the OECD embraced the growing concern among mainstream economists about rising inequality with the publication of a report entitled, *In It Together: Why Less Inequality Benefits All*, which focused on inequality in household disposable income. The report noted that in the mid-1980s, the Gini coefficient stood at .29, on average, across OECD countries. By 2013, it had increased by about 10 percent (or 3 points) to .32, rising in 17 of the 22 OECD countries for which long-time series are available (OECD 2015: 23). Of course, the average conceals variations between the most unequal countries (Chile, Turkey, and the United States) and the least unequal (Slovenia, Norway, and Denmark) (OECD 2015: 56). Inequality in Japan was somewhat above the OECD average, at .34 in 2011, the same as in the United Kingdom. In both countries inequality had risen from its level in the mid-1980s (OECD 2015: 24).

The OECD report was unusual in examining the interaction between the rise in interhousehold inequality and reductions in some dimensions of gender inequality in OECD labor markets. Rising female labor force participation contributed to narrowing the gender gap in paid employment in all OECD countries, in the period 1992–2013, to 16 percent, on average; however, because many women work part-time, the hours-adjusted employment gap was wider, at almost 24 percent. Among full-time employees, the gender wage gap, on average, fell 4 percentage points in the period

2000–2013, but women still earned 15 percent less than men, on average (OECD 2015: 32). The gender wage gap was highest in Korea, Estonia and Japan, at between 26.6 percent and 36.6 percent (OECD 2015: 213). Occupational sex segregation persisted, both horizontally in terms of sectors and vertically in terms of position in job hierarchies. Some 83 percent of women work in the service sector, compared to 34 percent of men. Only just over one-third of managers are women (OECD 2015: 213). Thus, even though the gender employment gap has fallen, there is still substantial gender inequality in the labor market.

The increase in women's labor force participation means that women's contribution to household income has risen on average. Using data from the Luxembourg Income Survey—which covers 20 OECD countries, but does not include Japan—the OECD report found that the proportion of households with a woman in paid employment rose, on average, from 52 percent in the mid1980s/early 1990s to 61 percent in the late 2000s. The proportion of households in which women work full time also increased, and so did the proportion with women in higher-paying jobs. The proportion of households with a woman working in a professional/technical/managerial job increased, on average, from 14 percent in the mid 1980s/early 1990s to 24 percent in the late 2000s (OECD 2015: 219).

The OECD report did not investigate the drivers of these changes, which might include, on the supply side, "distress sales" by women in low-income households, resulting from falling employment and/or wages of men in their households, and new aspirations for paid professional work by women in high-income households. On the demand side, drivers might include structural changes in production, with expansion of employment in sectors of the economy that are more likely to employ women, given the prevailing pattern of gender segregation, such as education, health and care services, and retail trade.

These changes clearly reduce inequality in earnings *within* households. OECD (2015) investigated their implications for income inequality *between* households. The impact of a reduction of gender inequality in labor markets on interhousehold income inequality might be to increase or decrease such inequality. For instance, if women taking up higher-paying jobs are primarily in households where men have higher-paying jobs, this would tend to increase income inequality between households. On the other hand, more women taking up full-time work in lower-income households might reduce inequality between households below what it would otherwise have been.

Using data from the Luxembourg Income Study, OECD (2015: 223–226) estimated what the Gini coefficient would have been in 2007 (or latest available precrisis year) if households had the same female employment characteristics as in the mid-1980s, and found that, overall, more women in paid work means less income inequality between households than would otherwise have been the case.

If the proportion of households with a woman in paid work had stayed as it was in the mid-1980s, the average Gini coefficient would have risen by an additional .8 points, from 28.2 to 31.6, instead of to 30.8. In some countries, the increase in proportion of households with women in full-time work is particularly important. For instance, in Canada, Ireland, the Netherlands, and the United States, the increase in women's full-time work is associated with a reduction in the Gini coefficient of between .6 and 1 points, compared to the Gini coefficient with no change. However, the increase in the proportion of households with women in higher-paying jobs is associated with a small rise in interhousehold inequality, .3 points, on average. But in almost all countries, the reduction of the gender wage gap on average served as a counterweight to rising household inequality. The combined impact of the reduction in gender inequality in labor markets reduced interhousehold income inequality below what it would otherwise have been, by about 2 Gini points on average. Thus, OECD (2015) found that reduction in gender gaps in employment and pay has mitigated, but has not outweighed, the tendency for income inequality between households to increase. The impact tends to be greatest where more women are employed full time.

This raises the question of whether the mitigating impact of the decrease in gender inequality in paid work is at the cost of more work in total for women, an extension of their total working day. Are women adding paid work to their existing unpaid care and domestic work for their families, or are men taking on more of this work, or are women in paid employment purchasing labor-saving technology or substituting paid services for their unpaid care and domestic work? The 2015 OECD study of income inequality did not examine inequality in unpaid work. The OECD Family Database does have some information on time spent in unpaid domestic work and care work,[5] but it is for latest available year in the period 1999–2012/2013 and does not have time series data. It has data for 24 OECD countries, including the United Kingdom and Japan. In all of them, women, on average, spend a greater share of the total time they have available (the 24 hours in each day) than men on unpaid domestic work and care work. For instance, in Japan men spend on average 4.7 percent of their time[6] on unpaid domestic work and .5 percent of their time on unpaid care work, whereas women spend 15.3 percent of their time on unpaid domestic work and 1.9 percent on unpaid care work. In the United Kingdom, men spend 9.5 percent of their time on unpaid domestic work and 1.6 percent of their time on unpaid care work, whereas women spend

16.6 percent of their time on unpaid domestic work and 3.6 percent on unpaid care work. Conversely, men spend a larger proportion of their time on paid work and study: in Japan, 26.3 percent, compared to 14.9 percent for women; in the United Kingdom, 20.1 percent compared to 11.9 percent for women (OECD Database Table LMF2.5.A).

Trends in women's shares of total paid work and of total unpaid work (domestic and care work) are presented by Gershuny 2018, using data from the Multinational Time Use Study, based at the Centre for Time Use Research at Oxford University. This includes most OECD countries but not Japan.[7] In most countries, women's share of paid work has increased from the mid-1970 s to around 2010, and women's share of unpaid work has decreased. But women still do between 60 and 75 percent of unpaid work.

Neither data on distribution of women's and men's time between paid and unpaid domestic and care work nor data on distribution of unpaid and paid work between women and men throw light on trends in the absolute amount of time women and men spend on these different types of work. Information on such trends for nonretired, nonstudent adults between ages of 21 and 65 in seven OECD countries (Australia, Canada, Finland, France, the Netherlands, Norway, and the United Kingdom) in the period from the1970s to the 1990s or 2000s was provided by Gimenez-Nada and Sevilla-Sanz (2012).

Except for France and the Netherlands, men decreased their paid work by an average of 4 hours and 45 minutes a week, which served to offset the increase in the time they devoted to unpaid domestic work (on average 3 hours and 35 minutes per week) and unpaid care work (1 hour per week). Men's total hours of work fell in Australia, Finland, and United Kingdom (calculated from Gimenez-Nada and Sevilla-Sanz 2012: 19, Table 3).

The experience of women was different. Women increased their paid work in six of the countries by an average of 6 hours and 35 minutes a week. The exception was Finland, where women already had the highest level of paid hours of work in the 1970s, but had reduced this by 5 hours and 15 minutes a week by the 1990s. Women also increased the time devoted to unpaid childcare in most countries, by an average of 1 hour and 20 minutes a week. Women did decrease the time they spent on unpaid domestic work by 5 hours and 45 minutes per week, but in most countries, this was not enough to offset the increases in time on paid work and unpaid childcare. In Australia, Canada, the Netherlands, Norway, and the United Kingdom, women's total hours of work went up (calculated from Gimenez-Nada and Sevilla-Sanz 2012: 19, Table 3). This suggests that in these countries the mitigating impact on interhousehold income inequality of reductions in gender equality in the labor market—which was particularly strong in the United Kingdom and Netherlands—came at the cost of more work in total for working-age women, on the average. Moreover, the data set used by Gimenez- Nada and Sevilla-Sanz (2012) did not take into account possible increases in the unpaid domestic and care work of women above the age of 65, as grandmothers take over some of this work formerly done by their daughters.

The OECD conclusion, "More women in paid work means less income inequality" (OECD 2015: 33) failed to examine the costs of women's increasing labor force participation in terms of the extension of women's total working day. Moreover, it did not examine what more women in the labor market means in terms of inequality between labor and capital. Much more of the income created as a result of increases in women's labor force participation may accrue to employers rather than to the households from which women come.

Decreasing gender inequality in labor markets but rising inequality between labor and capital

At same time as more women entered paid work, the share of national income going to labor in most OECD countries has decreased. In a pioneering study, using data for 1970–2000 for 23 OECD countries, Finnoff and Jayadev (2006) found that the female share of the labor force is robustly and strongly negatively correlated to the labor share of income (measured as ratio of compensation of employees to GDP, in which compensation includes wages and other benefits such as pensions). Controlling for factors such as GDP per capita, government share of GDP, trade taxes to trade ratio, capital account openness, unemployment, trade union membership, and ratio of part-time to full-time employment, they found that a 1 percent rise in the female share of the labor force is associated with a .2 percent to .6 percent decline in labor's share of national income. This negative relationship persists when the share of labor is adjusted to take account of self-employment.

It is important to take care in the interpretation of these results. There has been a longstanding fear in labor movements that women's entry into the labor market would undercut the bargaining power of male workers, and sometimes a wish to exclude married women from the labor force on these grounds. Finnoff and Jayadev (2006) did not conclude that there is an inherent and irreducible conflict between greater female participation in paid work and positive outcomes for workers. They noted the increase in competitive pressures arising from deregulation and globalization in the period covered by their research and suggested that, in the presence of continuing gender inequalities in labor markets, it is to the advantage of firms to use these inequalities in their interactions with labor. Such approaches, of course, can only work so long as these inequalities persist, and thus eliminating the disadvantages of women workers can serve to strengthen labor in the capital–labor relationship. Finnoff and Jayadev found that higher trade union membership is strongly positively associated with higher labor shares, which suggests that the more extensive and effective attempts to organize women workers would have a payoff not only for women workers but for men workers as well. Moreover, as Finnoff and Jayadev (2006) recognized, it may be the reduction in labor's share of income that has led to an increased participation by women in the labor force rather than vice versa. Declines in the bargaining power of labor may not only have reduced labor's share in national income but also caused more women to enter the labor force in order to compensate their households for the declines in men's real earning growth.

Complementary results have been produced by a study using data for private sector manufacturing, construction, utilities, and other services for 14 OECD countries in the periods 1970–2007 and 2008–2014 (Guschanski and Onaran 2017). It found a decline in the share of labor compensation as a ratio to value added, adjusted for labor income of self-employed, across the majority of these activities. This was found to be mainly attributable to offshoring production, a decline in the bargaining power of labor (as measured by union density, i.e., union members as proportion of workforce), and a rise in female share of hours of employment[8] (which is seen as a marker of lower bargaining power, given the disadvantaged position of women in the labor market) (Guschanski and Onaran 2017). Guschanski and Onaran concluded that an increase in the female share of employment in the absence of strong collective representation of women workers is associated with a fall in the wage share. This conclusion could be put on a firmer footing by disaggregating female and male union density, but data may not be easily available.

Braunstein (2019) investigated the relationship between labor share of income and female employment for developing countries in the period 1991–2014, using data from a variety of sources[9]. She made the innovation of trying to capture differential bargaining power of different groups of women workers by distinguishing women's relative share of industrial employment (as measured by the ratio of the proportion of women's employment that is industrial employment to the proportion of men's employment that is industrial employment) from women's relative employment for the economy as a whole (as measured by women's employment-to-population ratio divided by men's employment-to-population ratio). Her argument is that, in the context of industrializing developing countries, women have more bargaining power in industry than in agriculture or "traditional" services. The key results of this study are in Table 2.

Braunstein (2019) found that higher total employment for women relative to men is associated across all regions with lower labor shares, comparing early 1990s to early 2010s, although the association is stronger in Africa, Latin America, and the Caribbean than in Asia. For developing countries as a group, women's employment relative to men increased by an average of 8.9 percentage points over the period and correlated with as much as 95.5 percent of the decline in labor's share. However, there has been a decline in women's relative share of the industrial labor force, which is correlated with as much as half of the decline in labor's share for developing countries as a whole. But this correlation only holds at the regional level for Africa, Latin America, and the Caribbean, not for Asia, a region where the transition to high value added "modern" services is under way.

Although the two variables Braunstein used to try to capture differences in women's bargaining power in different kinds of employment are very broad brush, her results suggest that this is a fruitful approach that could be further refined, perhaps by looking at variables such as the share of women in public sector employment and share of women in nonstandard or vulnerable employment. She concluded that if women are integrated into labor markets on terms that are systematically inferior to men, capital tends to benefit by taking higher shares of revenues as profits, and wage shares get suppressed, ultimately worsening labor market outcomes for both women and men.

Strategies for reducing both gender inequality and class inequality

Fiscal policy does have an important role to play, and feminists are active in international networks pressing for tax justice (Nelson 2015). But as well as redistribution through the fiscal system, it is essential to change the operation of labor markets and the creation of productive assets. To reduce gender inequality and class inequality simultaneously, policy measures are needed to increase employment returns for low-income women. One important measure is to strengthen women's bargaining power by supporting trade unions and organizations of self-employed women. In fact, even though trade union membership in aggregate has declined, more and more women have joined trade unions. In 2012, women comprised the majority of trade union members in one-third of the 39 developing and developed countries for which data exist. In 16 countries, women comprised more than 40 percent of total union membership (Cobble 2012). Moreover, trade unions are focusing much more on issues vital for gender equality, such as equal pay, work–life balance, and gender-based violence at work. In addition, trade union organizing increasingly involves informal and migrant workers, homebased outworkers, and paid domestic workers (Pillinger and

Wintour 2018). Globalization has brought new challenges to traditional bargaining models, because they are based on national industrial relations frameworks, whereas a transnational response is now required across global supply chains. Global framework agreements have been negotiated to try to address this in sectors such as export-orientated horticulture, garments, and electronics (Pillinger and Wintour 2018). Nevertheless, the vast majority of women in paid work do not benefit from collective bargaining coverage, particularly in developing countries.

Legislating for minimum wages that provide a decent living wage may improve the pay of women who do not enjoy collective bargaining rights. But there are challenges in enforcing minimum wages for informal workers, who do not enjoy formal employment contracts. Thus, measures to promote formal contracts are important, such as the introduction of model contracts for paid domestic workers (OECD 2015: 39).

Expansion of public sector employment can increase returns for low-income women insofar as pay and conditions of work in the public sector are better than in the private sector. A study of the potential of public investment in public provision of care services for children and adults to create jobs for low-income women in seven OECD countries (Australia, Denmark, Germany, Italy, Japan, the United Kingdom, and the United States) found that investing 2 percent of GDP would create thousands of jobs that would most likely employ low-income women. In the case of Japan, estimates suggest that such investment would create about 1,313,500 jobs, about 77 percent of which would go to women; and in the case of the United Kingdom, it would create around 608,320 jobs, about 80 percent of which would go to women (ITUC/WBG 2016: 20–21). The same investment in construction would create about 1,052, 600 jobs in Japan and 287,450 in the United Kingdom, which would mainly go to men. As well as jobs directly created, there would be indirect creation of jobs through demand-side multiplier effects and supply-side input–output effects. The total job creation (including men as well as women) was estimated to be greater for investment in care than in construction. Investment in care services would raise the employment rate of women in both Japan and the United Kingdom by 5.1 percentage points, and for men by 3.4 percentage points in Japan and 2.3 percent in the United Kingdom (ITUC/WBG 2016: 26). Of course, with a higher level of investment, not only could thousands of jobs be created but the training, pay and conditions of care workers could be improved to recognize that provision of high-quality care is a skilled task.

Public investment in care services has the potential not only to create more and better jobs for low-income women but also to address the root causes of low-income women's weak position in the labor market, which lies in their continued disproportionate responsibility for ensuring the care of their families and communities. Such investment reduces women's unpaid care and domestic work (Elson 2017) and strengthens their bargaining position in the labor market.

It also contributes to the creation of collectively owned assets in which returns accrue to users of services for which they are not charged the full cost. Building support for public investment in collectively owned assets is critical for the reduction of both gender and class inequality, creating a counterweight to privately owned assets. It is important to create more of a sense that citizens own collective assets by setting up democratic systems for their management, involving both users and producers (Elson 1988). Piketty was right to draw attention to the increasing concentration of ownership of private assets, and the returns to such ownership do need to be more effectively taxed; but we also have to put back on the agenda the redistribution of assets. Focusing on provision of care—for children, for adults with chronic ill-health and disabilities, for elderly people—is a good place to start building a persuasive case for the creation of collective assets that would help to secure a reduction in both gender and class inequality.

Notes

1. Income is only one dimension of class. Occupation, education, and property ownership are other important dimensions.
2. For instance, as explained in the introduction of the book, Piketty (2014: 17–18) used data from income tax and estate tax records
3. Feminist economists regard skill as a problematic category. Identification of work as "skilled" tends to depend on social and economic power; and formal educational qualifications often serve, at least in part, as gatekeepers to entry into better-paying jobs. Tacit skills, which are acquired through experience, tend not to be recognized. Women tend to acquire tacit skills of various kinds through the way they are brought up in their families and communities, which prepares them for jobs requiring diligence, patience and empathy (see, e.g., Elson and Pearson 1981).
4. This article defines unpaid work as unpaid care and domestic work, following the terminology adopted internationally in the United Nations Sustainable Development Goals: Goal 5.4
5. OECD groups time use in six broad categories: work-related activities, unpaid work, care work, personal care, leisure, and unspecified time. The category "unpaid work" includes unpaid domestic activities such as cleaning, washing, repair work, shopping, and volunteer work but not time spent exclusively caring for a child or another person, and broadly corresponds to the concept of "unpaid domestic work" as used by the United Nations. The OECD category "care work" is unpaid time exclusively spent caring for a child or another adult, regardless of whether they live in the same household. This broadly corresponds to the concept of "unpaid care work." The OECD categories can be confusing, as much care work is paid and would be included

in "work-related activities" for people employed in private and public sector institutions.

6. In this paragraph, "their time" refers to the 24 hours in the day.
7. The Statistics Bureau of Japan has not made the time use data it collects available for inclusion in the open access data base of the Centre for Time Use Research, University of Oxford.
8. This is a better measure of female share of employment than female share of the labor force, as it takes account of fact that not all women participating in the labor force are employed, and many who are employed work part-time hours
9. Data on labor shares from Penn World Tables; on employment from ILO, World Development Indicators, and UN Statistical Division.

References

Baumol, W. 1967. "The Macroeconomics of Unbalanced Growth." *American Economic Review* 57 (3):415–26.

Beneria, L., and G. Sen. 1982. "Class and Gender Inequalities and Women's Role in Economic Development: Theoretical and Practical Implications." *Feminist Studies* 8 (1): 157–76. doi:10.2307/3177584.

Braunstein, E. 2019. "Gender-inclusive Industrialisation for Growth and Development in the Context of Globalization". In *Gender Equality and Inclusive Growth. Economic Policies to Achieve Sustainable Development*, edited by D. Elson and A. Seth (pp. 76–106). New York, USA: UN Women.

Cagatay, N., D. Elson, and C. Grown. 2000. "Introduction -Growth, Trade, Finance and Gender Inequality." *World Development* 28 (7):1145–56. doi:10.1016/S0305-750X(00)00032-2.

Cagatay, N., D. Elson, and G. Grown. 1995. "Introduction: Gender, Adjustment and Macroeconomics." *World Development* 23 (11):1827–36. doi:10.1016/0305-750X(95)90003-J.

Cobble, D. S. 2012. *Gender Equality and Labor Movements: Toward A Global Perspective.* Washington DC: Solidarity Centre.

Elson, D. 1988. "Market Socialism or Socialization of the Market." *New Left Review* 172: 3–44.

Elson, D. 1998. "The Economic, the Political and the Domestic: Businesses, States and Households in the Organisation of Production." *New Political Economy* 3 (2):189–208. doi:10.1080/13563469808406349.

Elson, D. 1999. "Labour Markets as Gendered Institutions: Equality, Efficiency and Empowerment Issues." *World Development* 27 (3):611–27. doi:10.1016/S0305-750X(98)00147-8.

Elson, D. 2017. "Recognize, Reduce, and Redistribute Unpaid Care Work." *New Labor Forum* 26 (2):52–61. doi:10.1177/1095796017700135.

Elson, D. Ed. 1991. *Male Bias in the Development Process, Chapters 1 and 7.* Manchester, UK: Manchester University Press.

Elson, D., and R. Pearson. 1981. "Nimble Fingers Make Cheap Workers: An Analysis of Women's Employment in Third World Export Manufacturing." *Feminist Review* :87–107. doi:10.2307/1394761.

Finnoff, K., and A. Jayadev. 2006. "Feminization and the Labor Share of Income." GEM-IWG (The International Working Group on Gender, Macroeconomics and International Economics) Working Paper 06-4. University of Utah: Department of Economics.

Folbre, N. 1994. *Who Pays for the Kids? Gender and the Structures of Constraint*. London, UK and New York, USA: Routledge.

Galbraith, J. K. 2014. "Unpacking the First Fundamental Law." *Real-World Economics Review* 69 (7):145–8.

Gershuny, J. 2018. "Gender symmetry, gender convergence and historical work-time in 25 countries." Presentation to Conference of International Association for Time Use Research, Budapest. https://www.iatur.org/page/40th-iatur-conference

Ghosh, J. 2014. "Piketty and the Resurgence of Patrimonial Capitalism." *Real-World Economics Review* 69 (7):138–44.

Gimenez-Nada, J., and A. Sevilla-Sanz. 2012. "Trends in Time Allocation: A Cross Country Analysis." *European Economic Review* 56 (6):1338–59. doi:10.1016/j.euroecorev.2012.02.011.

Guschanski, A., and Ö. Onaran. 2017. "The political economy of income distribution: industry level evidence from 14 OECD countries." Greenwich Papers in Political Economy., University of Greenwich, #GPERC51.

Harvey, M., and N. Geras. 2018. *Inequality and Democratic Egalitarianism*. Manchester, UK: Manchester University Press.

Heintz, J. 2019. *The Economy's Other Half*. Newcastle Upon Tyne, UK: Agenda Publishing.

Himmelweit, S. 2007. "The Prospects for Caring: Economic Theory and Policy Analysis." *Cambridge Journal of Economics* 31 (4):581–99. doi:10.1093/cje/bem011.

ILO. 2013. *Global Wage Report 2012/13: Wage and Equitable Growth*. Geneva: ILO

IMF. 2017. "Fostering Inclusive Growth." *Note Prepared for the G20 Leaders' Summit, Hamburg*. Washington DC: IMF.

ITUC (International Trade Union Confederation)/WBG (Women's Budget Group). 2016. *Investing in the Care Economy*. Brussels: ITUC.

Nelson. L. (ed.). 2015. *Tax Justice Focus- The Gender Issue*. 10 (1). http://www.taxjustice.net/2015/05/14/tax-justice-focus-the-gender-edition/

OECD Family Database, OECD Social Policy Division- Directorate of Employment. Labour and Social Affairs. http://www.oecd.org/els/familydatabase.htm

OECD. 2015. In *It Together: Why Less Inequality Benefits All*. Paris: OECD.

Oxfam. 2017. "An economy for the 99%." Briefing Paper. London: Oxfam.

Pearson, R., and D. Elson. 2015. "Transcending the Impact of the Financial Crisis in the United Kingdom: Towards Plan F- a Feminist Economic Strategy." *Feminist Review* 109 (1):8–30. doi:10.1057/fr.2014.42.

Perrons, D. 2014. "Gendering Inequality; A Note on Piketty's Capital in Twenty-First Century." *British Journal of Sociology* 65 (4):667–77. doi:10.1111/1468-4446.12114.

Picchio, A. 1992. *Social Reproduction*. Cambridge: Cambridge University Press.

Piketty, T. 2014. *Capitalism in the Twenty First Century*. Cambridge, Massachusetts: Harvard University Press.

Pillinger, J., and N. Wintour. 2018. *Collective Bargaining and Gender Equality*. Newcastle upon Tyne: Agenda Publishing.

Stockhammer, E. 2013. "Why have wages shares fallen? A panel analysis of the determinants of functional income distribution." Conditions of Work and Employment Series No 35. Geneva: ILO.

UNDP. 2015. *Humanity Divided: Confronting Inequality in Developing Countries*. New York: UNDP.

The reproductive crisis in neoliberal capitalism: Commenting on D. Elson's recent paper

Makoto Itoh

ABSTRACT
In the first section, this paper comments favorably on Elson's recent paper applying the "gender lens" to rising economic inequalities under neoliberal capitalism. Although increased participation of women in the labor market reduced economic inequalities within and between households to some extent, it widened the income gap between capital and labor. I note and comment on similar trends in the Japanese economy. In the second section, this paper examines how to reread Piketty as "patrimonialism without patriarchy" in light of Elson's critique. In the third section, the widening economic and gender inequalities are located as an important link in the vicious circle of reproductive crisis of our societies, with suggestions for a sounder theoretical foundation and possible strategies for dealing with such crisis for the future.

"Gender lens" applied to expanding economic inequalities under neoliberal capitalism

Diane Elson's paper, "Intersection of gender and class in the distribution of income" (2019) applies a "gender lens" (3)[1] to the analysis of rising economic inequalities under neoliberal capitalism as a critique of Thomas Piketty (2014). Although Piketty attracted wide attention to the reemergence of inequality of wealth and income in advanced economies under neoliberalism, he focused primarily on the concentration of wealth (or capital) among the richest 1–10% of people at the expense of the assets of the middle class. Elson's gender lens goes beyond this broad-brush view by pointing out that the income gap between labor and capital under neoliberalism rose, paradoxically, alongside an increase in women's participation in the labor market.

Elson has had a long-standing theoretical interest in the Marxian labor theory of value (as shown in Elson (1979, reprinted 2015), to which Nobuharu Yokokawa and I contributed an essay) and it serves, alongside the gender lens, as a frame of reference for her critique of Piketty. In Marx's theory, unlike in classical or neoclassical economics, wage labor is not a natural form of labor, but one generalized historically only in capitalist societies. Even so, capitalist enterprises actually prefer wage labor mainly in the urban manufacturing, commercial and financial sectors. They tend to leave many other sectors, such as peasants farming, small family businesses and unpaid domestic work, to non-wage labor. This sort of non-wage labor serves to form industrial reserve armies that can be mobilized when needed. It gives greater flexibility to the labor market.

Contrary to the general impression, capital has not failed to mobilize women wage labor through most of its history. Since the beginnings of the industrial revolution in the UK, capitalism mobilized women and child workers massively in the cotton industry as Marx (1867) described in chapter 15, "Machinery and Large-scale Industry," of *Capital*, Volume 1. However, as heavy industries became the leading sector of economic growth in the late nineteenth century, male workers were increasingly preferred. They set the ruling norm of the male breadwinner of the ideal modern family in which women after marriage were housewives doing unpaid domestic work. That is why in addition to the demand for universal suffrage, a key demand of women's liberation movements in the following decades was for greater women's participation in the labor force. It was seen as constituting liberation from being mere housewives confined to unpaid domestic labor.

Unexpectedly, this demand was most substantially realized in the four decades of neoliberalism under the impact of ICT (information and communication technologies), which spread automation to both factories and offices. It was part of a larger restructuring of capitalist economies after the inflationary crisis of 1973–1975 that ended the high economic growth in the postwar long boom. The result was, according to Elson (2019), citing an OECD (2015) report, that "rising female labor force participation contributed to narrowing the gender gap in paid employment in all OECD countries, in the period 1992–2013, to 16%, on average. However, because many women work part-time, the hours adjusted employment gap remained wider, at almost 24%. Among full-time employees, the gender gap fell, on average, 4% points in the period 2000–2013, but women earned 15% less than men on average" (8).

In the case of Japan, in the period 1973–1996, female employment increased 75.1% from 11.9 million to 20.8 million, while male employment increased 33.3% from 24.3 million to 32.4 million. Thereafter male employment decreased to 31.3 million by 2010, while female employment continued to increase to 23.3 million to reach around three quarters of male wage workers. Clearly considerable feminization of wage labor has thus taken place and almost doubled female employment since 1973. Dual income families have become rather usual. Japanese women's labor market participation rates by age groups used to form an M shape curve, initially rising with age, then sharply declining in the group 25–29 years old due to marriage, childbearing and rearing, then rising again before declining with retirement. It has now become a less pronounced M shape as the age group representing the trough moved from 25–29 to 30–34, and further 35–39 years old and the trough itself became shallower since the 1990s (cf. Itoh, 2000, 63).

Nevertheless, many women work part-time, just like in other OECD countries. In 2011, irregular female employment in part-time, temporary and dispatch work, generally with much lower wage rates and often without the fringe benefits that regular workers get, amounted to 11.88 million or over one-half of total female employment in Japan.[2]

Clearly, increased female participation rates in labor market under neoliberal capitalism did not end the patriarchal oppression of women as early women's liberation movements expected. As Elson stresses in her paper, although it certainly reduced gender inequality within many households, and to some extent served to mitigate inequality between households, it did not much diminish patriarchal gender discrimination in the labor market and the workplace. It also clearly tended to prolong women's total labor time in both unpaid domestic and wage labor.

Furthermore, as Elson notes, increased female participation in the labor market seems to have accompanied decreases in labor's share in national income in most OECD countries. However, the causality here is complex and Elson criticizes Piketty for reducing it to the lower marginal productivity of female labor. Marx had long ago suggested a theoretical possibility for reducing the value of labor-power by dividing it among more family members mobilized for wage labor. As he put it, "machinery, by throwing every member of that family onto the labor-market, spreads the value of the man's labor-power over his whole family. It thus depreciates it" Marx (1867, 518). Theoretically, trade unions might be able to avoid or mitigate such changes by organizing a sufficient portion of wage workers. However, in many OECD countries, such as the USA, Germany and UK, except some northern European countries, the rates of trade union membership in total employed workers tended to decline under neoliberal policies promoting privatization of public enterprises, deregulation of labor laws to enable diversification of irregular forms of employment, and the globalization of capitalist investment to utilize cheaper workers abroad. With this trend unions' socio-economic power to defend labor conditions and real wage rates have been weakened.

Especially in Japan, as a corollary of the Japanese style of management, most trade unions were company unions traditionally organizing mainly male regular employees in the same company. As a result, they could not effectively organize increasing women irregular workers and have had to lose both organization rate (proportion of union labors in total employed workers) and social power to defend their wages and working conditions under neoliberalism. Japanese organization rates in total employed workers thus continuously declined from 35.4% in 1970 to 24.2% in 1993, and further to 16.7% now in 2019. As Elson suggests recent efforts to organize part-time workers in many advanced economies have had some success and the Japanese organization rate of part-time workers is also increasing, though it still remained at just 8.1% in 2019.

As a result, real wages in Japan became very stagnant in the 1980s and have even tended to decline since the 1990s, contributing to chronic deflation. The gap between rising physical labor productivity by means of ICT automation system and this trend in real wages must work unfavorably for the labor share of national income. In fact, the Japanese labor share has declined particularly steeply since the 1990s, reflecting the trend in other OECD major countries (Tanaka, Kikuchi, and Ueno 2018). One must note, however, that this trend is considerably weaker than the decline from 75% in national income to 65% between the mid-1970s and the mid-2000s in a group of developed countries as mentioned in Elson's paper referring to a UNDP (2015) report.

If we consider the non-labor share in national income to be roughly equal to the capital share or profit share, as Elson does, why did the Japanese capital share not increase more despite real wages lagging far behind the continuous increase in physical labor productivity by means of ICT at workplaces? The answer must include the unfavorable impact of repeated rises of the yen against dollar, suppressing the profits of exporting industries until the early 1990s, the increasing competition of the rapidly growing manufacturing industries in developing countries in both global and domestic markets, and the prolonged deflation. In addition to these factors restricting Japanese profit shares, there is, of course, the manipulation of business accounts to hide profits through accelerated depreciation, higher investment costs, sales costs, and research and development costs in order to escape or reduce corporation tax.

In fact, the total amount of retained earnings in Japanese corporations continuously increased during the long deflation to reach around 463 trillion yen in 2018 maintaining or pushing up the asset value of corporations. In the meantime, the total number of low-income households that now qualified for welfare assistance was estimated to reach 11.05 million or 22.3% of total households in 2002, in which 6.2 million (18% of working households) were working poor households. Only 15–20% of this total low-income households could receive public welfare assistance, thanks to difficult application processes and severely controlled approvals limited by the narrowly restricted welfare budget.

Thus, Japanese society, which had once become quite egalitarian in terms of the distribution in income and wealth in the period of high economic growth, reversed the trend. This pattern confirms Elson's main line of argument against the OECD's analysis of intersecion of class and gender which concludes that "more women in paid work means less income inequality," and against Piketty's negligence of the gender issue. As Japanese historical experience also demonstrates, increased women's participation in wage labor ironically worked unfavorably for the labor share of national income thanks to continuing patriarchal gender discrimination at workplaces (while most of trade unions that did not support struggles of women workers or try to organize them also in a patriarchal way) combined with the burden of unpaid domestic labor, and obviously widened economic inequality among people, especially by spreading new forms of poverty such as that of the working poor under the neoliberal capitalist order.

How to re-read Piketty

Elson's critique of Piketty's analysis in *Capital in the Twenty-First Century* through her gender lens is summarized as "patrimonialism without patriarchy" (4). It contains rich historical and theoretical insights on at least three issues.

Firstly, as is well known, Piketty statistically demonstrated that inherited wealth in major capitalist countries remained steady at 6–7 times the annual national income between the 18th century and the beginning of the 20th century. It declined to 2–3 times in the period from 1914 to 1970 and rose again to the previous level in the U shape curve after the 1980s. Japan is a typical case. If such inherited wealth, whether in the form of real estate such as land or other capital assets brought in 4–5% return (as non-labor income), as Piketty assumes, assets valued at 7 times the national income can easily enable its owners to obtain 28–35% of national income as profit share.

We note, along with Elson, that such a patrimonial socio-economic order was also patriarchal especially in the pre-World War I period, as women had fewer inheritance rights, and men controlled the property of their wives. As women gained suffrage, however, such legal gender discrimination including unequal inheritance rights was mostly eliminated in advanced countries in the latter half of the 20th century.

Therefore, Elson recognizes that patriarchy today is more subtle and is not rooted in lack of legal rights but social norms assigning unpaid care and domestic work to women and confining the majority of women to low-paid, low-status occupations.

Thus, secondly, Elson criticizes Piketty's negligence of the role of patriarchal gender discrimination in increasing inequality within labor incomes in favor of "meritocratic" salaries of super-managers. As she emphasizes correctly that though care work, for example, requires many tacit skills that women acquire at home and school, it tends generally to be lowly paid in labor markets under the social norms that discriminate against women's work.

As we have seen in the first section, according to Elson's analysis, increased female participation in the labor market worked to reduce the gender income gap within households and between households to some extent. However, it did not resolve the gendered discriminatory norms and practices in the labor market and paradoxically worked unfavorably for the labor share as a whole. By using the gender lens, her paper explored the weakness in Piketty's analysis of the resurgence of economic inequality under neoliberal capitalism. In focusing on the revival of patrimonial inherited wealth concentrated in the top 1–10% of the rich, he neglected the role of more subtle patriarchal gender discrimination in labor market.

Thirdly, in combination with these two issues, Elson challenges Piketty's "implacable logic" that inequality will rise so long as rate of return on "capital" (asset or wealth) (r) is greater than the national economic growth (g), or $r > g$. If the long-run rate of return to "capital" assets remains at 4–5% as Piketty assumes, the wider decline in the rate of economic growth (or of real national income) due to slower growth in productivity and demographic change after the period of high economic growth in the postwar long boom must increase capital's share.

Against Piketty's logic, Elson's gender lens shows how the social reproduction of labor "shapes both the rate of economic growth and the rate of return on capital, ... through complex, historically specific, and contradictory processes, not through 'implacable logic'" (6). This argument should be supplemented by three further points.

First, Piketty has no theoretical explanation for determining the rate of return on capital and he does not clarify why the long run rate of return tends to persist at 4–5% for so long and across different historical periods. In neoclassical economics, the marginal rate of profit is generally assumed to be identical with the rate of interest, without showing an objective source of profit. According to Boehm = Bawerk's subjective and theoretically weaker time preference theory, however, profits depend on the psychological preference for present consumption over future consumption. The degree of preference for present consumption may go down (even to zero) when productivity growth reduces (even to zero). Schumpeter therefore introduced the role of innovation as a stimulus to gain profit for investment. However, technological and managerial capitalist innovation cannot theoretically be guaranteed to occur so constantly and evenly to assure 4–5% capital profit as Piketty assumes.

In my view, Piketty's assumption of the long run constant average rate of return on capital is not based upon conventional theories of interest and profit in neoclassical economics. Rather it is obtained from recent historical series of national income accounting. From these measures, the return on capital or economic surplus is deduced by subtracting labor income from total social product and the rate of return on capital is then calculated as the ratio between this surplus to total national wealth. The way in which capital extracts a profit is better explained by the labor theory of value in Marxian political economy which succeeded the classical school and saw profits originating from social surplus labor time beyond labor time necessary to reproduce labor power through capital-labor market relations.

Second, although profits are indeed a constant rooted in the exploitation of wage labor as recognized in Marxian economics, it does not follow that the rate of return must be constant. As Elson correctly argues, it can be altered through complex social processes including the historical, political and social factors that determine labor time socially necessary to reproduce labor power. The degree of strength of workers' struggle, for instance, may affect the length of working day as Marx pointed out. The standard of consumption, the goods and services considered necessary for generational reproduction of labor power also varies historically. Under neoliberal capitalism along with increased participation of women in wage labor, the labor share has deteriorated (and the rate of exploitation has correspondingly increased) owing primarily to restructuring of economies and globalization, and to patriarchal attitudes of employers and traditional trade unions.

Elson's analysis must be extended to confirm the direction and degree of change in the rate of return. Unlike the neoclassical tradition, in Marxian political economy the rate of profit on actual (industrial, commercial and services) investment is determined by the technical conditions and the value of labor power, factors distinct from those that determine the rate of interest. Low rates of interest since the 1990s are not, therefore, evidence of a lowered rate of return of real business investment in the form of operational profit or rent.

Third, Elson does not merely criticize Piketty for ignoring the intersections of gender and class in the distribution of income. Her critique is directed also at Piketty's main line of argument about the causes of inequality. While not negating the importance of Piketty's statistical discovery of the remarkably constant capital share, she provides a fuller analysis of the phenomenal recovery of capital in our age of neoliberal capitalism.

Piketty's somewhat abstract and ahistorical "implacable logic" of rising inequality in the distribution of wealth arising from the widening gap in the formula $r > g$ where r remains relatively stable, as well as his meritocratic view of labor income must be criticized. As Elson suggests, r and g as well as evaluation of the value of labor power in market are determined through complex socio-political factors that include gender bias and public policies of the state. If the rate of return on capital did not decline much despite lower economic growth rates in the neoliberal era, there must have been an overall increase in surplus value or profit and a reduction in the labor share with a series of structural change and globalization besides increasing participation of female labor in market, as Elson analyses, and through widespread reductions in corporation and inheritance taxes for richer persons. Unlike in the previous era of high economic growth until the early 1970s, such increasing profit was not re-invested in industrial expansion so as to expand employment and increase real wages proportional to labor productivity. Instead they were saved as internal reserve assets in corporations or served to increase financial and real estate assets and thus the greater wealth of richer persons.

The reproductive crisis in neoliberal capitalism to be challenged

Rising inequality of wealth and income is thus analyzed by Elson as a social result of four decades of neoliberal capitalist accumulation using subtle patriarchal gender discrimination in wage and non-wage labor to reduce the labor share of the whole working class. The resultant increase in the wealth of the top 1–10% has not been useful for economic growth or stability.

The economic growth rate of major advanced economies slowed down more and more and is approaching zero or turning negative, reflecting the constriction of consumer demand. Instability of employment and economic life of the mass of the people has clearly intensified as a series of speculative financial bubbles have burst. Under the circumstances, capitalist firms have tended to rely on more and more female cheap irregular workers by means of ICT automation systems, forming a vicious circle of deflation. The Japanese economy famously experienced such a vicious circle in the lost three decades after the collapse of huge bubble in 1990.

Amid this deflation, the social reproduction of labor, "the core of feminist understanding of the economy" (6), has also failed, forming an important link in this vicious circle. In many advanced economies, declining birthrates and ageing populations threaten the recovery of economic growth along with the reproduction of laboring population. For instance, typically in Japan, women's total fertility rate (TFR or an average life-long birth-rate per woman) declined from 2.14 in 1973 to 1.26 in 2005, below the 2.1 necessary for simple reproduction of population. This was the so-called "1.26 shock." The TFR then recovered a little to 1.45 in 2015, as the postwar junior baby-boom generation took their last chance to have children. However, this was temporary and the Japanese TRF is sliding down again.

According to a statistical estimation released in April 2017 by Japan National Institute of Population and Social Security Research, Japan's population will decline 30% in 50 years from 127.09 million in 2015 to 88.08 million in 2065. The Japanese population decline had started already after the peak year 2008 (when it was 128.08 million) and will be halved by the end of this century and will go further down to its pre-Meiji Restoration Edo period size by the end of next century. As the proportion of the elderly increases, the social costs of supporting their pension, health insurance, and care services must increase the public burden on the shoulders of the working population who face a dismal future of diminished public support when they need it in turn. Although the average number of working people supporting an elderly retired person was still 7.7 in 1975, it declined to 2.6 in 2010, and will be less than 2 after 2020, though this may be offset by raising the retirement age probably but to a limited extent.

Anxiety about the economic future among the younger generation has also been intensified by the ecological crisis, including global warming generating abnormal weather and floods. Furthermore, the recent giant earthquake and tsunami inducing the dangerous destruction of Fukushima nuclear power generation plant as we experienced in Japan 2011, as well as recent corona pandemic crisis all reveal fundamental fragility and vulnerability of social reproduction of people's lives in neo-liberal competitive capitalist market order while declining fertility may help to offset ecological crisis by reducing consumption over the medium run but not surely and sufficiently.

Thus, we have to conceive of ways to challenge the increasing economic inequalities under neoliberal capitalism as part of a larger strategy to resolve the multiple crises endangering social reproduction of population itself. New ideas and conceptions for 21st-century models of socialism in the broad sense including social democracy are globally needed and gathering attention.

Piketty's proposal of international cooperation to set up a tax on capital assets can mitigate the concentration of wealth among the top 1–10%. However, promoting such a policy requires the social power and organization of trade unions and working people to be reconstructed by organizing more female irregular workers into unions as Elson points out. Gender biased discrimination of women in wage labor with an excessive burden of unpaid domestic work combined with discrimination in the labor market should be overcome in order to increase the labor share against capital share through the unionized struggle of both female and male workers.

In this regard, I am afraid that even a feminist demand for equal wage for equal work may imply approval of meritocracy in the male-dominated labor market for skilled or complex labor. It will only import into the female labor market differentiated reward for different kinds of complex labor which has never had much objective foundation. In the long tradition of Marxian feminist political economy, the issue of how to value different degrees of skilled useful concrete labor as homogeneous abstract human labor time has not been given a satisfactorily egalitarian resolution. It is because most Marxian value theorists followed an aspect of Marx's theory of complex labor to conceive (just like Smith and Ricardo) that an hour of skilled labor is socially equalized or reduced to more hours of unskilled simple labor (Chuma 2017).

As Marx (1867, 135) did not present a complete theory to explicate the "social process that goes on behind the backs of producers" to determine the proportions in which different kinds of complex labor are reduced to simple labor, there appeared two influential streams of interpretation, as I argued elsewhere (Itoh 1988, 6.1).

One of them, exemplified by I. Rubin (1972) takes the view that the estimation of skilled labor as abstract human labor can be arrived at only through pricing its products or services in the market. This type of interpretation contradicts the basic logic of Marx's theory of value which explains relative prices of commodities from the basis of the objective labor time they embody and constitutes a circular explanation. It can also permit meritocratic evaluation of labor time in accord with pricing in the market and will not permit simple aggregation of women's market and non-market labor time as homogenously abstract human labor comparable with men's' labor time as in Elson's critical analysis in the paper we are commenting on.[3]

The second interpretation, that costs of educating and training skilled workers result in an elevated value of skilled labor-power being transferred to its products, is also unsatisfactory. The value of labor-power, unlike the value of machinery, is not transferred to the product, but must be reproduced by living labor as expenditure of the use-value of the commodity labor-power in Marx's theory. In addition, this interpretation also tends to admit a kind of meritocracy privileging complex labor time according to the educational and training costs. So long as educational and training costs for elite professional careers are enhanced more and more with neoliberal privatization policies that cut public support for universities, the social reproduction of such complex labor is limited to richer families as Piketty

(2014, 486) pointed out. A practically feudal hereditary social reproduction system of elites reappears with reduced social mobility ironically under a neoliberalism allegedly committed to competitive freedom in a capitalist market economy liberated from social restrictions and hierarchies.

Such additional education and training costs borne individually must enhance the value of skilled labor power in order to assure the generational reproduction of skilled workers necessary for society through the market economy. However, it is highly dubious whether such skilled workers' labor is objectively more intensive and heavier in comparison with various kinds of simple labor which also often requires a combination of various human skilled activities, as Elson emphasizes in case of care work. If all the educational and training costs for necessary skilled workers are totally socialized and free in a social democratic or socialist society, it may not be fair to estimate skilled labor time with higher remuneration in comparison with the same length of simple labor.

Thus, apart from the value of skilled labor power in capitalist (not socialist) reproduction system of labor power, the expenditure of skilled labor power as a use-value need not be differentiated from simple labor. In this regard, Marx's proposition, following Smith and Ricardo, that an hour of skilled labor should be estimated as multiples of an hour of simple labor had better be revised, based on Marx's own more fundamental original notion of dual character of labor. According to Marx, the human labor process, unlike other animal's instinctive activity, must conceive its result in advance and realize this conception purposefully through concretely useful forms of labor to produce various use-values of products. Even the various kinds of simple labor involved in care work can be regarded as a concrete form of human abstract capacity of labor, which is potentially "a whole world of productive drives and inclinations" (Marx 1867, 481) in each individual person, in common with the skilled complex labor.

If we can thus appreciate that complex labor is essentially homogeneous abstract labor applied to special concrete forms, we can easily overcome meritocratic overestimation of skilled wage labor.

As Elson pointed out in her paper "Market socialism or socialization of the market" (1988), the reproduction of labor-power, including child care and education, must be socially guaranteed in a socialist society. Corresponding to this, the effectiveness of expanding public investment in care services for children and adults, health care and medical services, free access to higher education and training as well as to internet (web) utilities is to be highly recommended to resolve excessive economic inequalities including gender bias which endanger the social reproduction of the laboring population.

In order to promote these alternative strategies, we probably need to consider further how to achieve really democratic socialization of the reproduction of labor-power from the grass-roots in ways that go beyond the limitations of 20th-century statist nationalistic models of socialism and social democracy. Besides the restoration of the regulatory role of central government over services for social reproduction of laboring people, as suggested by Elson, international workers' cooperative movements and decentralized and democratic local governments are necessary. At the same time social and community organizations such as trade unions, workers and consumers cooperatives, regional currencies, and other mutual assistance community organizations, as well as various people's dissident social movements must broadly be encouraged to prepare and create the 21st-century models of social democracy and socialism from below.

We have argued that complex labor is essentially abstract human labor equally commensurable with simple labor in composing total social labor time necessary for our economic life. We have also argued that that the meritocratic evaluation in wage labor, which often includes gender bias, the more or less arbitrary estimation of educational and training careers, and the tendential negligence of non-wage domestic labor must thus be avoided. These arguments must offer a theoretically sounder foundation for the social movements mentioned above and for attempts to prepare and achieve a more egalitarian economic democracy based upon labor time as Marx expected.

Acknowledgments

Let me state here my sincere gratitude for cooperative editorial advices, comments and revisions of expressions in English offered to refine this paper by Dian Elson, Radhika Desai, Nobuharu Yokokawa, and anonymous referees.

Notes

1. Citations from Elson (2019) are indicated just page numbers in this paper.
2. As for references to Japanese historical experiences throughout this paper, see also more detail in Itoh (2000, 2013).
3. Chuma (2017) criticizes Rubin's theory of abstract labor and its influence in misguiding some feminist analyses on the economic distinction and relation between wage labor and non-wage domestic labor.

References

(For books and papers in Japanese, the titles are translated into English in square brackets.)

Chuma, S. 2017. ["Equality of Human Labour within Our Economy in the Broad Sense"]. *Political Economy Quarterly* 53 (4):62–73.

Elson, D., ed. 1979. *Value: The Representation of Labour in Capitalism*. London: CSE Books. Reprinted 2015 by London: Verso Books.

Elson, D. 1988. "Market Socialism or Socialization of Market." New Left Review. https://newleftreview.org/issues/i172/articles/diane-elson-market-socialism-or-socialization-of-the-market.

Elson, D. 2019. "Intersection of Gender and Class in the Distribution of Income." *The Japanese Political Economy* 44 (1):7–24.

Itoh, M. 1988. *The Basic Theory of Capitalism*. London: Macmillan and New York: Barnes & Noble.

Itoh, M. 2000. *The Japanese Economy Reconsidered*. Houndmills, Hampshire: Palgrave.

Itoh, M. 2013. *[Why Japanese Economy Has Withered?]* Tokyo: Heibonsha.

Marx, K. 1867, 85, 94. *Capital, I, II, III*. Transl. by B. Fowkes and D. Fernbach. Harmondsworth, UK: Penguin, 1976, 78, 81.

OECD. 2015. *In It Together: Why Less Inequality Benefits All*. Paris: OECD.

Piketty, T. 2014. *Capital in the Twenty First Century*. Cambridge, MA: Harvard University Press.

Tanaka, G., Y. Kikuchi, and Y. Ueno. 2018. ["Analyses of Factors for Recent Declining Rate of Labour Share"]. A Discussion Paper, Japan Economic Research Bureau, March. Tokyo: Cabinet Office.

UNDP. 2015. *Humanity Divided: Confronting Inequality in Developing Countries*. New York: UNDP.

Index

Note: Figures are indicated by *italics*. Tables are indicated by **bold**. Endnotes are indicated by the page number followed by 'n' and the endnote number e.g., 20n1 refers to endnote 1 on page 20.